UNDERTHROW

HOW JEFFERSON'S DANGEROUS IDEA WILL SPARK A NEW REVOLUTION

MAX BORDERS

SOCIAL
EVOLUTION

CONTENTS

PREFACE

Every normal man must be tempted, at times, to spit on his hands, hoist the black flag, and begin slitting throats.
—H. L. Mencken

Imagine a gorge cut ages ago by the river Time. Two tribes live, one on either side of the gorge: the Reds and the Blues. A thick rope connects the two tribes as each pulls in a seemingly endless game of tug-o-war. The walls of the gorge are steep. When one side starts to gain an advantage, tuggers from the other side fall into the river below. Those who remain tug harder, so they start to gain an advantage.

This game has been going on for so long that few question it.

Behind each tribe, ghoulish spectators yell, "Pull!" from comfortable perches. The ghouls promise goodies to the tuggers should their side win. Some tuggers fall with a splat onto the muddy banks that flank the river. A few land in the water and get carried away by the current. Dirty and disheveled, fallen tuggers from team Red or Blue make their way back to shore, then climb up the winding trails to the back of the tug-o-war line. There they find a length of rope waiting. Despite being scratched, bruised, and muddy, they again hear the ghouls yell, "Pull!"

So they pull.

A few just watch the whole thing with disgust. Occasionally, an onlooker joins in the tug-o-war. Otherwise, they shake their heads. Some tuggers have been dragged into the mud enough that they refuse to participate. All this pulling for Red or Blue seems pointless, especially for those with Purple or Green sensibilities.

"If you don't pull the rope, you have no right to complain," say the Blues.

"Pulling for Purples or Greens is wasted effort and ensures Blue wins," say the Reds.

The Blues' general hypothesis is that one day, their team will muster the strength to pull all those horrible Reds into the gorge once and for all. The Reds' general hypothesis is that one day, their team will muster the strength to pull all those horrible Blues into the gorge once and for all. Both sides agree they have to recruit bystanders to win, even though the game offers little to the bystanders. It's winner-takes-all for Red or Blue, so *pick a team.* Or so the theory goes.

Enter the Blackshirts.

The thing about Blackshirts is they never pull the rope. Blackshirts earn their color because they question the whole god-damned thing. So, of course, the Reds and Blues reject them utterly. But the Blackshirts are clever. They know that tug-o-war is wasteful. Indeed, the rope stays taut because both sides pull so hard. How might that fact be exploited?

What if, one day, the Blackshirts decided to shimmy out onto the rope, each with a dagger in clenched teeth? The Reds *and* Blues would want to stop them, but they couldn't. If either side lets go of the rope to go after the Blackshirts, the other side would gain the advantage. So they would keep pulling while yelling curses at the Blackshirts, who would ignore the obscenities. Some Red or Blue ghouls would no doubt hurl stones at the Blackshirts. But maybe there would be enough Blackshirts for one to make it. If one succeeded in cutting the rope, the Reds and Blues would fall. The tug-o-war would be over.

The point of this colorful allegory is simple: This book is for Blackshirts. It's not just a call for readers to don subversive colors. As H. L. Mencken wryly put it in the quote above, we yearn to fly the black flag (better, of course, to cut ropes than slit throats). Blackshirts earn their colors because, like Mencken, we remain skeptical of the whole bloody enterprise. We must therefore muster the courage to climb out over the gorge. And cut.

For too long, we've been fattened on a steady diet of civic lore about democracy, but that system only helps lock partisans in perpetual warfare. The war is meant to settle two questions: Who gets the resources? And who gets control? Each team holds out hope that one day, they'll get to shove the *One True Way* down everyone's throats. They just have to pull harder.

Blackshirts see things differently.

I wrote this book because I am a pamphleteer by nature. When I look at the absurdity of the world around us, I imagine how Thomas Jefferson and old Tom Paine must have felt. I have an obligation to expose the absurdities, articulate the alternatives, and call others to action.

Where there was once civic consciousness among the people, there is now little but partisan animus. Despite widespread attachment to voting and elections, innovators are figuring out better ways to organize themselves outside tug-o-war politics.

The only way to win is to play a different game.

INTRODUCTION

The tree of liberty must be refreshed from time to time with the blood of patriots and tyrants.

—Thomas Jefferson

Nonviolence is a weapon of the strong.

—Mohandas Gandhi

When Jefferson wrote the words in the above epigraph, he was in France. He had written a letter to William Stephens Smith, the son-in-law of John Adams. Jefferson worried that his compatriots were making too much of this whole business of putting down rebellions.[1] Just twenty-two years before, he had helped inspire an uprising of his own. Jefferson saw this rabble with their pitchforks and muskets as the last stand against the powerful.

"And what country can preserve its liberties," he wrote, "if their rulers are not warned from time to time that their people preserve the spirit of resistance?"[2]

Jefferson was a revolutionary. Some, like the little-known twentieth-century anarchist Voltairine de Cleyre, thought Jefferson was nigh an anarchist despite his serving as Secretary of State and two terms as President. To channel J.R.R. Tolkien, Jefferson resembled not a whiskered-men-with-bombs anarchist but rather a skeptical-of-authority anarchist. De Cleyre saw in the American colonists a tradition of mischief-making against the powerful:

> The revolution is the sudden and unified consciousness of these traditions, their loud assertion, the blow dealt by their indomitable will against the counterforce of tyranny, which has never entirely recovered from the blow, but which from then till now has gone on remolding and regrappling the instruments of governmental power, that the Revolution sought to shape and hold as defenses of liberty.[3]

How long and to what extent can the instruments of governmental power be used to defend freedom before the powerful degrade those instruments and turn them on the people?

Such questions troubled Jefferson. Far from warming him to power, Jefferson's own political life seemed to stiffen his skepticism.

"Never did a prisoner, released from his chains, feel such relief as I shall on shaking off the shackles of power," wrote Jefferson in a separate letter.[4]

Still, one can imagine poor William Stephens Smith

receiving Jefferson's tree-of-liberty missive and thinking the statesman somewhat flip about bloodshed. But in 1787, the threat of popular uprisings was the last check after all other measures had been exhausted. In some respects, it still is. The goal of the American Whigs had been to *overthrow* the tyrants, at least on American soil.

In an 1887 letter to Madison, Jefferson wrote of three primary societal forms—no government, participatory governments, and governments of force. The third, he thought, "is a government of wolves over sheep."[5] The second, he believed, "has a great deal of good in it."[6]

But the first?

"It is a problem not clear in my mind that the first condition is not the best."[7]

We need not take Jefferson's anarchistic streak as illiberal or disorderly. We need only show that he and the antifederalists were right to warn us about the Constitution. In fact, they were downright prescient. With the arc of history bending as it has, we can still have Jefferson as a main character in the American story without committing to any principle of periodic bloodshed. And that's where *underthrow* comes in.

But first, a detour.

FROM SUBJECT TO CITIZEN, CITIZEN TO CUSTOMER

One thing Whig's adversaries couldn't stand about them was their whiggish insistence on the march of progress. Their idea of progress was not like the fever dreams of modern progressives, but rather a belief in the inevitable improvement of society through time. The horrors of the twentieth century militate against the idea of inevitable progress. Yet progress has directionality. Despite lurches, detours, and cycles of decline, humanity tends to transmit—and build upon—knowledge. The totality of that knowledge includes recipes for improving our lives.

Humanity benefits from the collective intelligence embedded in the simplest things—including this very page. Happily, there are compounding returns to knowledge, especially when entrepreneurs offer to instantiate recipes in the form of products and services. We can consistently access such bounty thanks to competitive markets. For example, few of us know how to build a set of headphones. Despite our relative ignorance of electroacoustic transducers, most of us get to enjoy music.

Because knowledge is distributed among billions of people worldwide, it's the job of entrepreneurs and innovators to put together the people and resources necessary to unlock that knowledge and build on it for society's benefit. But society isn't a monolith. It is a complex churn of competing perspectives, preferences, and needs.

Educational entrepreneur Michael Strong postulates a law to this effect:

Ceteris paribus, properly structured free enterprise always results, over time, in higher quality, lower cost, and more customized products and services.[8]

Strong's Law applies in areas people traditionally think of as firewalled from enterprise, such as *governance* and *welfare* functions. Strong argues that, far from being segregated from the market process, visionary entrepreneurs would radically improve these areas in a milieu of competition.

So, my related hypothesis is:

Society will evolve towards greater peace, freedom, and flourishing to the extent that people treat other people as customers—instead of citizens or subjects.

The claim, bold but tentative, is that if the market is a decentralized discovery process, surely we can use it to discover better social systems. In seeing governance as transactional instead of transgressive, a million possibilities arise. Yet status quo bias prevails. It's hard to imagine governance innovations not yet born. Can't we imagine creative founders blazing new trails?

I realize that, for many readers, this thesis might be a record-scratch moment. After all, didn't Aristotle say that a citizen is a person who possesses the virtues of ruling and being ruled? He did, but please hold your tomatoes. The great political scientist Vincent Ostrom warned that "the most radical source of inequalities in human societies is the "ruler-ruled" relationship."[9] Ostrom argues that those who want a truly free world must figure out how to build fundamental infrastructures that allow people to govern themselves.[10] We shouldn't forget that true self-government had been the Founders' ultimate objective, too. De Cleyre reminds us that, beyond the battles they fought:

[T]he real Revolution, was a change in political institutions which should make of government not a thing apart, a superior power to stand over the people with a whip, but a serviceable agent, responsible, economical, and trustworthy (but never so much trusted as not to be continually watched), for the transaction of such business as was the common concern and to set the limits of the common concern at the line of where one man's liberty would encroach upon another's.[11]

Such an inversion had been exceptional in human events, launching new republics. But as power accretes around a central authority, its dark gravity builds.

So, what does all this have to do with viewing citizens as customers?

Most associate the word *customer* with commerce rather than politics. Our mandarin class will no doubt also associate the word with something bourgeois and spiritually hollow, like a used-car salesman who wants you to buy a lemon. But consider three basic ways an individual can relate to a separate organization:

- If the primary relationship is one of obedience, then one is a *subject*.
- If the primary relationship is obedience behind a thin veil of voting, then one is a *citizen*.
- If the primary relationship is one of consent, then one is a *customer*.

Abstracted away from the dirty traffic of the merchant classes, most people can appreciate that consent is the healthiest way to relate to other human beings. Indeed, we might find it useful to map the above relationships onto Jefferson's three types of society I mentioned above. In so doing, we can sacralize the word *customer* more than we do—at least allowing it to have one foot in the profane and the other in the sacred.

Consent is the key.

Whatever the stories we were told in civics class, when too

much of society gets built on the interests of a ruling class, citizens and subjects become an afterthought. That is, if, as citizens, we have no choice but to associate with a coercive state bureaucracy, the question is: Why? Is it because taxing authorities—people with guns and jails—force our compliance? Otherwise, why can't you or I *choose* to associate with an organization, say, a provider of governance services? If we did, wouldn't we expect good service, especially if such service were our counterparty's contractual obligation?

Unhappy customers can take their business elsewhere.

Persuasion and coercion are fundamentally different kinds of relationships between people. The health or dysfunction of society gets determined largely by the relative mix of these. It would seem that good governance must arise from the political realm and not the commercial. But couldn't that just be a story the powerful have always needed us to believe? And do great swaths of humanity believe the political is primary because they imagine that justice originates in something other than human choices? Otherwise, we must confront the possibility that the need for coercion is a story we tell ourselves, especially those who want to impose their moralisms onto others.

Either way, I suspect most of us have been sold a bill of goods by would-be philosopher kings.

New vectors of change, unavailable to the American Founders, allow us to become a countervailing force without violence. We must never forget, then, that we launch our attacks against unjust authorities from the highest ground of all: *consent*. Our enemies have to operate from the low perch of compulsion.

UNDERSTANDING UNDERTHROW

It's a coincidence that the title of this book sounds like another word, but it turns out the coincidence is fruitful.

Think of the sea at night. The moon reveals the surf's fury, which pounds the dunes and sprays the beach. What monsters lurk beyond the waves? What slithers beneath the foam? The swimmer fears the answers, but as she enters the water, an undercurrent recedes as new waves approach. She's nearly swept off her feet.

That's *undertow*.

It's powerful, so much so that more swimmers should fear it, though too many underestimate its power. They focus on those crashing breakers, full of sound and fury. And so do our enemies.

Underthrow includes undertow.

Like receding ocean waters, we can start to appreciate how unexpectedly powerful we can be when we retreat from the status quo together. Like water molecules, we must find each other, bind together, and flow like dark waters rushing back into the deep. We are not supremely powerful, but powerful enough to topple giants.

CONSENT AS MEANS AND END

We've already seen that consent is vital. We know at least that, in its absence, we get compulsion. It seems reasonable to think that the use of compulsion by any person against another ought to have limits, especially if we're talking about mere humans compelling other humans who have done no wrong.

So the first thing to stress is that consent is both an *objective* and a *strategy*. Consent is an objective in that, following Jefferson, we seek a consent-based social order. Consent is a strategy because, increasingly, it is possible to make societal change through a series of implicit or explicit agreements. In fact, the more parties to an agreement, the more formidable the constituency.

Take the simple example of software development. With open-source code, software developers organize themselves into teams to make useful software product *x*. The teams organize themselves this way because they have a shared mission. Yet the end product is not proprietary. It's controlled and developed by a community of people who share a commitment to a common mission, so there has to be a consensus mechanism for making unitary decisions on behalf of the group.

But software developers have disagreements, especially when it comes to what direction the development community will take to realize the mission. If a major disagreement can't be resolved within the community, some subset of developers will splinter off. Such is known as a *hard fork*. When there is a hard fork, the splinter group of developers makes a copy of the existing codebase and changes it as they see fit, but they leave the original codebase unchanged. The team that remains continues in the way they see fit, as well. The result is two competing software products. When the competing forks launch, users have the option of choosing which product they want to use.

Why can't society be this way?

That is the question before us and, in great measure, the *raison d'etre* of this book. But before we close this introduction, I want to emphasize that underthrow has a psychological dimension. Some might even call it spiritual. Pluralistic governance is liberation technology, and liberation is not just a process. It is a psychosocial end state that peaceful people crave. Underthrow is thus subversive social change. Whether you share values with the left or the right doesn't matter. Left/right is not the relevant axis for questions of consent.

Anti-authoritarians operate on a different axis, as we'll see.

LOCALISM

Most reform efforts start small or local, or both small and local. As Voltairine de Cleyre reminds us:

> Among the fundamental likeness between the Revolutionary Republicans and the Anarchists is the recognition that the little must precede the great; that the local must be the basis of the general; that there can be a free federation only when there are free communities to federate; that the spirit of the latter is carried into the councils of the former, and a local tyranny may thus become an instrument for general enslavement.[12]

But enough anarchist talk. After all, even non-anarchists can get behind the idea of community and local authority. Much like the word *liberal*, the A-word has been abused, appropriated, and bastardized to the point that the simple concept—of rules without rulers—has been lost. Noam Chomsky identifies as an anarchist, for heaven's sake.

"Localism does not claim to be able to produce a Utopia through means of government," writes author Mark Moore. "Rather, it claims to be the best way to protect us from the delusions of madmen..."[13]

There is something about localism that cuts through the fog. We all understand intuitively that we can be more helpful to our neighbors, demand accountability from our leaders, and enjoy the fruits of cooperation when the most important decisions stay with our communities. That's because individualism is communitarian.

We trust the institutions we choose to build together.

DAMN LIBERALS

When your crazy uncle listens to conservative talk radio and shakes his fist at the American left, what does he call them?

Whether an adjective or noun, "liberal" in today's parlance means the opposite of conservative. To hear a partisan tell it, liberal or conservative is the only game in town. The history of this meaning stretches back to the early twentieth century when progressives poached the word in an act of political legerdemain. As political theorist Linda C. Raeder notes, the misappropriation goes back at least a hundred years.

"The American people generally warmed to the term liberal," writes Raeder. "Thus they could be swayed to support Progressive proposals labeled as such."[14]

By the 1920s, *New York Times* editors damned "the expropriation of the time-honored word "liberal" and demanded that "the radical red school of thought... hand back the word to its original owners.'"

You read that right. *The New York Times.* What a difference a century makes.

Verily, I don't relish the idea of devoting any more ink to the task of explaining what I mean when I use the word *liberal,* but we mustn't forget that our crazy uncle might need straightening out. So to reclaim the word, we ought to have our definitions in order. Whenever you read the words *liberalism* or *liberal* in this volume, I refer to freedom's doctrine or those who embrace it, respectively.

The original word indicates something very different from its modern mutation, referring to people of a different moral sensibility and intellectual outlook. They used to call liberals Whigs, but God help whoever tries to resurrect that homely term. In any case, true liberals had become increasingly rare as the administrative state grew to become the object of admiration by an aspirational elite. As the economist Dean Russell wrote in 1955:

It is true that the word "liberal" once described persons who respected the individual and feared the use of mass compulsions. But the leftists have now corrupted that once-proud term to identify themselves and their program of more government ownership of property and more controls over persons. As a result, those of us who believe in freedom must explain that when we call ourselves liberals, we mean liberals in the uncorrupted classical sense. At best, this is awkward and subject to misunderstanding.[15]

The right has also contributed to such misunderstanding. Conservatives, especially those in the traditionalist mold, practically sneer the word. The late Rush Limbaugh turned it into a slur throughout the 1990s and 2000s, so much so that many on the left scurried back to the term "progressive" despite that term's sorry association with eugenics and economic planning.

Though I have never been much for tacky jingoism, I have always admired the American founders. King George III called them the "American Whigs." This improbable group of polymaths was liberal in the truest sense: *Libertas perfundet omnia luce.*

Freedom will flood all things with light.

WRITTEN TO INSPIRE

Humanity has yet to realize its potential. Therefore, my ultimate purpose for this book is not to startle you with controversy but to inspire you. We must break out of our comfortable confines and shed our psychological servitude. Only then can we build a new society. Following Jefferson, Paine, and Spooner, I hope this book will rouse a new generation of revolutionaries committed to a specific form of nonviolent action, which we call underthrow.

In Part One, I set out the *absurdities* of our current situation. In Part Two, I raise vital questions about *alternatives* to the status quo. Finally, I sketch out a series of *actions* commensurate with underthrow in Part Three.

Before you continue, the question is whether you might be fearful, complacent, or have different allegiances. The fearful have a strong submission instinct only they can overcome. This book can help. The complacent refuse to see the looming dangers. This book can help. Those allied with the powerful stand in the way of liberation and progress because they stand to gain. This book cannot help them, for they are the giants in the surf. Despite the risks of ugly criticisms and one-star ratings, I hope to persuade the fearful and the complacent to find the courage to join up with us anti-authoritarians—if not for us, for our children.

Underthrow is for the brave, the determined, and the free.

PART ONE
ABSURDITIES

1

THE CHURCH OF STATE

The urge to save humanity is almost always only a false-face for the urge to rule it.
—H. L. Mencken

DARKNESS DESCENDS over civilization and freedom. It flows not from any external threat but from within the human heart. We are beings capable of happiness and flourishing, but sometimes we push our fears and anxieties into the shadows. There they fester. And from those deep psychological bowers, the fear and anxiety reemerge transformed. It makes people do stupid things, like giving power to bad people.

To live right now, then, is to live in paradox. Despite conditions of relative peace and abundance, a psychosocial pathology has taken hold. It manifests itself as something like a replacement religion. Where people once turned to their temples and communities for reassurance, more turn now to political authorities.

Merchants of fear magnify frictions and tragedies for our entertainment. They obscure complicated truths and feed this new faith's dogmas. Adherents believe they are on the side of the angels, but their faith threatens to bring about a new Dark Age. Why? Because more and more people in the grip of this religion are willing to use illiberal means in service of their ends.

Exitus acta probat.

THE RISE OF THE CHURCH OF STATE

It's no secret that Americans are losing their religion—particularly the young. And despite being an unbeliever, I can say that I'm not sure this has altogether been a good thing.

According to Gallup, only 47 percent of Americans attend a church, synagogue, or mosque, which is down from 73 percent when the pollsters first asked the question in 1937.[1]

Despite humanity's history of religious wars and persecutions, most major religions offer some moral guidelines —virtues, values, and guidance on how to live a good life. Variations of the Golden Rule appear in almost every faith. But as more Americans have left organized religion, they have also abandoned a source of moral teaching and moral community.

Nature abhors a vacuum, the saying goes. So, where are these lost souls turning for their morality in the absence of religion?

As people have become less religious, they have transferred their need for its trappings into the political realm. That religion, which I call the Church of State, offers people three Articles of Faith:

1. *Prosperity as Immorality* is the notion that our abundance is the product of our sin;

2. *Society by Design* is the idea that society and
   economy can be administratively ordered by
   elites; and
3. *The Authoritarian Urge* is the will to control
   others, whether to quell our fears, overcome sin, or
   force one's ideals into existence.

Now, cross these Articles of Faith with *three big problems*, and you can see how this new Church of State currently organizes itself:

Wealth Inequality. One sect is obsessed with the idea
that some people control considerable resources while
others have too little. Such obsession causes the
adherents to focus on what the rich have rather than
what the poor lack. They seek *equality of outcomes*,
which means using illiberal means to confiscate wealth.

"Inequality is the root of social evil."
—Pope Francis.

Climate Emergency. Another sect is preoccupied with
an impending apocalypse due to energy consumption,
which leads to runaway warming. Positive climate
feedback loops will eventually cause fragile ecosystems
and societies to collapse. They seek *climate stability*,
which requires the abrupt curtailment of production
and consumption.

"This is the biggest crisis humanity has ever faced"
—Greta Thunberg.

Social Injustice. The third sect fixates on the idea of

justice as a cosmic scoreboard. They think neutral, liberal rules not only perpetuate racism but allow the privileged to preserve their power over oppressed minorities. They seek *equity*, which means using illiberal means to right historical wrongs or correct perceived power imbalances.

"One either allows racial inequities to persevere, as a racist, or confronts racial inequities, as an antiracist."
—Ibram X. Kendi

The most powerful aspect of the Big Three problems is that each has a grain of truth: Some rich people have gotten richer through a rigged game, and poor people continue to struggle; climate change is occurring to some degree, and we have all contributed to it; certain people benefit from a legacy of slavery and Jim Crow, while overt racists gather and march from time to time. These are all problems that people of conscience should come together to address.

But those dedicating their lives to the Big Three tend to exaggerate their severity. Indeed, the most zealous put these issues at the center of all moral, social, and economic life. Once they are there, no other concerns or values matter. And that monomania changes one's ideological priors into religious dogma, particularly when people organize around that monomania.

Consider how the Articles of Faith intersect with the Big Three Problems.

	Prosperity as Immorality	Society by Design	The Authoritarian Urge
Wealth Inequality	Because people are primarily greedy, wealthy societies are disastrously unequal, which means unfair and unjust.	There is an ideal distribution of resources and wealth in society; we must design society to realize that ideal.	Those who control excess wealth and capital must be brought down a peg or two through wealth distribution.
Climate Emergency	Because consumers are greedy, they use too much energy and release too many greenhouse gases, hastening a crisis.	There is a mix of personal commitments and renewable energy mandates that will save us all.	Industrialists drive catastrophe, so authorities must regulate them at any cost, even to economic growth.
Social Injustice	Because the powerful and the privileged are mostly greedy, they will oppress minorities to preserve their privilege.	Use state power to bring about ideal social justice, including reparations, quotas, and unequal treatment.	Intersectional power must ascend to dismantle the power and privilege of the oppressor class by any means.

When we were in a global pandemic, it would have been tempting to add that dynamic into the mix. After all, the pandemic of 2020–2022 stoked widespread fear and anxiety to the point that, for many, totalitarian measures have become palatable. But concerns about public health, like the pandemic itself, were transitory. People moved on. "Irish Democracy," that general unwillingness of the people to comply, eventually overwhelmed the political class.

In other words, concerns about viruses, though real, didn't have the same durable features as the Big Three simply because inequality, climate change, and social injustice deal in abstractions. The claims are more difficult to falsify. That makes solving such problems much harder, but converting people to the Church of State far easier.

Thus:

There is no vaccine for racism. So we place our faith in something else: We have to "do the work" of antiracism, which means certain groups must first confess to the Original Sin of privilege. These sinners must then allow an enlightened ruling class to launch illiberal measures to dismantle "white supremacy," which is *everywhere*. Only then can they atone.

There is no drug for the climate emergency. So we place our faith in global bodies and confess the related sins of consumerism and corporate greed, which threaten to boil our fragile ecosystems. The sinners must then allow an enlightened ruling class to control the means of production and curb consumption. Only then might the climate crisis be averted.

There is no herd immunity for inequality. So we place our faith in politicians promising to deal with the billionaires building space toys as the homeless wander the streets of San Francisco. The sinners must allow an enlightened ruling class to confiscate wealth so that the poor get housing, the hungry get fed, and sociology majors get student loan forgiveness.

THE COMMON DENOMINATOR

Before we explore more detailed outlines of an evolving religion, have you noticed the common denominator in what we have set out so far? You. Your sins. And, of course, mine. Together, our sins—vaguely defined, collectively held, and impossible to shed—are systemic racism, energy consumption, and greed. Systemic racism means no one is allowed to take personal responsibility for the sins of the past, say, through the practices of color blindness or demands for equal treatment. Energy consumption means that creating a modestly comfortable life for you and your family is something shameful to be corrected. And if you decide to save and invest rather than spend and waste, you are responsible for contributing to a grotesque wealth gap.

The only path to absolution is your abject humility before the Church of State. What does that look like in practice? It looks like you and I are on our knees before armed tax and regulatory authorities who were once activists—acolytes of this new triune God.

OUTLINES OF A RELIGION

By now, hopefully, you're starting to see the outlines of this new religion coming into view. To make it starker, consider how the new religion maps onto features of an older one:

> Omniscience. *The entity is all-knowing. Install the most devout of the flock and trust in them. If you don't, you have simply lost faith, which you must regain.*
>
> Omnipotence. *The entity is all-powerful. Therefore, it can solve all social problems, as long as the benighted are out of the way and the enlightened are empowered to realize its plans.*
>
> Enlightened vs. Benighted. *There is a special class of people who possess correct opinions. That class's work is to shed light on those still in the dark.*
>
> Impending Apocalypse. *If we do nothing— where "we" refers to authorities—x will happen, which will result in humanity creating hell on earth.*

Heaven Awaits. *There is a better society just waiting for the enlightened class to conceive, design, and build it for everyone else. First, we must all give up our own plans. Then we must acquiesce to the planners' designs.*

Original Sin. *A mysterious force keeps us from doing the right thing, and, in many ways, it always has. It is not really in our control to change, but we must confess our sin, then self-flagellate.*

Good vs. Evil. *Those who agree with us are good. Those who do not are evil.*

Indulgences. *You can atone for sin if you give financial support to the right authorities. This will eventually translate into social good, and you and subsequent generations will someday arrive at a better condition.*

Faith vs. Reason. *Eschew evidence, rationality, and neutral discourse. Instead, embrace talking points, narratives, and "lived experience."*

Asceticism and Self-Flagellation. *You are born evil. To cleanse yourself, you must deny yourself pleasure and self-administer pain so that you never forget you are weak and flawed.*

The Priesthood. *You should follow and recite the proclamations of the most well-known and active among the enlightened class. Be among the herd.*

Sacred and Profane. *Some places symbolize that which is pure, and other places symbolize that which is morally depraved. (DEI spaces*

are sacred. *Nature is sacred. The gas pump
and fast food restaurant are profane.)*
Embodied Evil. *If an omniscient and
omnipotent entity represents the good, then a
powerful, countervailing entity must
embody the evil.*
Blame and Shame. *If the unbelievers cannot yet
be coerced, one must hector them. They will
eventually identify with us, if not to assuage
their guilt, then to get on the* right side of
history.
Messianic Figure. *Occasionally, someone appears
who promises to save us. The priesthood must
rally around this figure so that the laity
will too.*
Scapegoat. *Someone or something, who
symbolizes Sin, has to be destroyed.*
Victimhood as Virtue. *Victims of oppression or
"the system" are incapable of responsibility
or wrongdoing.*

One could go on: There are chosen people, eschatologies, and methods of converting those who risk damnation. And as with the above list, individual members of each sect might differ in terms of which of the Big Three they reference. One wonders if such differences create the conditions for a schism.

SCHISM OR SCAPEGOAT?

This religious order is holding itself together, but that could change. After all, in most religious orders, there is *One True Way.* Whether that way lies in the pieties, rites, and liturgies a sect adopts—or in determining what particular sin is most egregious—the more differences each sect finds in the details, the more they will see the other sects as competitors.

To maintain unity, it might not be enough that all the sects worship in the Church of State. They might have to maintain unity through the sacrifice of a common scapegoat. And that scapegoat could well be you, Dear Reader.

I don't suggest such things to strike fear in anyone. Instead, we should consider that it might be time to create another form of civil association into which a new generation can transmit and then transmute their fears. Because if I'm correct that the Church of State is the apotheosis of people's transferred anxieties, then they will always be looking for an outlet— whether in government power or something else. The State is a fundamentally violent institution, so we should fear it most of all, even if "our team" happens to be in office for a term.

We must also be concerned about vengeful reactions within the Church of State because reactionaries seek to put down their enemies. Such reactions risk turning the rest of us into collateral damage in a twenty-first-century civil war.

What must we do?

We must upgrade our liberal humanism. We must upgrade our social operating system. And we must upgrade ourselves. We do so by integrating ancient wisdom with modern innovation. We must attain a liberal humanism that unifies people in the secure bosom of community, rooted in our human natures, and expands our pluralism.

Finally, in viewing one another as sacred entities, even the godless might find something closer to divinity. If we don't embrace a doctrine of sacred persons, we risk returning to the horrors that marked the twentieth century.

"Never again," we promised. But only in freedom can we keep that promise.

2

POLITICS IS THE PATHOLOGY

In vain you tell me that Artificial Government is good,
but that I fall out only with the Abuse. The Thing! The
Thing itself is the Abuse!
—Edmund Burke[1]

THERE'S NO MORE exciting and anxious time in an author's life than launch week. The book you've spent nine months writing and three months editing will be revealed.

When I launched my last book, *The Decentralist*,[2] my very first reviewer gave the book one star out of five, writing:

> Though I found some information useful, and the author's initial intentions as shown in the introduction resonating [sic], a large part of the book has to do with self-created morality and meaning, which sounds a lot like an anti-government + new age cult.

Ouch. That stung.

I'm reminded of the editor's admonition: It's not about what you intend but how readers receive your work. Now, instead of me arguing with this reviewer about what he got wrong, I'd rather talk about what he got right—notwithstanding the one-star rating. At the risk of taking more lumps, I hope the idea challenges readers.

AN ANTI-GOVERNMENT NEW-AGE CULT

That reviewer's description, though hyperbolic, contains a grain of truth. In other words, *The Decentralist* was designed to read like the text of a secular religion. Jeffersonian esoterica. I knew I was taking a risk, but I had to try.

You see, elsewhere I had lamented the loss of religious affiliation in America, not because I'm a fundamentalist, but because I worry that such a loss has led to a decline in an essential source of community, moral teaching, and social feedback.[3] Religious affiliation had been a last redoubt after the decline of the mutual-aid sector.

Today we see the consequences of this decline.

I also worry that, for most, there is no going back to that old-time religion. But most religions share important patterns. Sometimes, we can borrow from them. Still, those who have strayed from their flocks are experiencing civic, moral, and spiritual malnourishment and we cannot sustain social coherence with politics alone. Yet people are projecting politics onto morality's magisterium, where it doesn't belong. They resist any admonitions around such a projection, as politics offers a hollow kind of identity for many.

Before we move on to the idea that politics is a domain

distinct from morality, I should briefly address a couple of points.

First, my work is not precisely "anti-government," but it will almost certainly come across that way to people who worship in the Church of State. More subtly, it is both anti-authoritarian and communitarian. In other words, instead of One Ring to bind us, there should be many rings. Instead of one all-powerful Nation-State, many smaller cultural and governance niches should offer us entry and exit options. Instead of One Imperial Power to force the *One True Way*, there should be competing, self-organizing jurisdictions that can function as independent experiments. These can rise or fall according to their ability to attract and retain ~~citizens~~ customers (or members if you prefer).

Let a thousand systems bloom. Let us vote with our feet.

What better way to create local experiments than to provide opportunities for people to *opt out of—and into—* different systems? Localized experiments that fail are preferable to national experiments that end in catastrophe. This idea is radical, but it isn't new. That's why I base it on a more familiar piece of secular scripture, a passage that bears repeating in this volume:

That to secure these rights, Governments are instituted among Men, deriving their just powers from the **consent of the governed**—That whenever any Form of Government becomes destructive of these ends, it is the Right of the People to alter or to abolish it, and to **institute new Government**, laying its foundation on such principles and organizing its powers in such form, as to them shall seem most likely to effect their Safety and Happiness.

I'm sure King George III thought this revolutionary poppycock was positively New Age at the time. But in building on the Founders' wisdom, my goal is to inspire readers to finish the Revolutionary project, whether in America or abroad.

But first things first.

THE SIX SPHERES

A people's health lies in each person's commitment to being good. The ancients referred to virtues because these were moral commitments to be practiced, not just abstractions plucked from the air. Elsewhere, I identify such virtues as Six Moral Spheres:

1. **Nonviolence**—to refrain from making others worse off in their person, property of exercise of will
2. **Integrity**—to be of one's word and to honor one's commitments
3. **Compassion**—to be attuned to others' value as individuals and thus to their suffering
4. **Pluralism**—to be tolerant of others' perspectives and to seek facets of truth in them
5. **Stewardship**—to take care of one's property or offices, leaving them better off
6. **Rationality**—to seek truth by employing the facilities of reason

One might not consider the Six Spheres sufficient, but they are essential for maintaining a society of peace, freedom, and abundance. So when my reviewer says I'm flirting with "self-created morality," I can agree to the extent that, without conscious, continuous practice, our moral universe starts to disappear. We must continuously create the moral universe through our *actions*. But I ain't making this stuff up. The Six Spheres are timeless.

2000 years ago, the Indian sage Patanjali compiled the Yoga Sutras, which one might describe as a guide to a good life, a series of aphorisms on the theory and practice of yoga. Included in those practices are the Yamas, or rules of right living. In Sutra 2.35, Patanjali writes:

---

ahimsā-pratiṣṭhāyām tat-sannidhau vaira-tyāgaḥ

This translates from Sanskrit as: "In the presence of one who is firmly established in nonviolence, hostility recedes." Such wisdom is intuitively true. Being around a someone who radiates peacefulness can help us be peaceful, too. Maybe that's why ahimsa, or nonviolence, is the bedrock of three religions: Hinduism, Jainism, and Buddhism.

Five hundred years before Patanjali, in Babylon, a descendent of the house of King David, Rabbi Hillel the Elder, said famously, "That which Is hateful to you, do not do to your fellow! That is the whole Torah; The rest is interpretation."

The ancients are trying to tell us that being good is about action. It takes work, not just lip service. It takes practice, not just social media posturing. And vitally, the fruits of being good require solidarity among people in a moral community. The community's members can enjoy the benefits when more members practice (consequentialist ethics). Individual members can flourish together in becoming more excellent (virtue ethics). Any given member should respect these universals as duties we have to each other (deontological ethics). As you can see, I don't care much about theoretical arguments about which of these ethical forms ought to prevail among philosophers. Instead, let them be woven together as a braid—and practiced.

THE SIX OFFENSES

Now, the Six Spheres have *vicious mirrors*, practices that can *destroy* the social order. The Six Offenses are as follows:

1. **Violence**—To threaten or initiate harm against others to compel them in some way
2. **Corruption**—To use unscrupulous means to some end, such as wealth or power
3. **Callousness**—To show indifference to the suffering or plight of others
4. **Monomania**—To labor under the idea that there is One True Way and no other
5. **Negligence**—To shirk one's responsibility to care for her offices or property
6. **Casuistry**—To employ specious or deceptive rhetoric instead of good discourse

Those who worship in the Church of State think of the Six Offenses not as immorality but as strategies. The ends justify the means. Indeed, the Centralist thinks policycraft is the sum of morality and the end of political strategy. Morality gets reduced to a plank in a partisan platform. Far from being immoral, destructive, or "vicious," as we might urge, The Six Offenses are just how the sausage gets made.

But, the following insight is falsely attributed to social theorist Marshall McLuhan:

We shape our tools, and then our tools shape us.

Similarly, I argue that,

We shape our rules, and then our rules shape us.

The more we reduce moral practice to political strategy, the more we create moral malignancies out of bad rules.

Violence. Consider that the entire edifice of the nation-state exists because a group of elites control a monopoly on violence. This is an undeniable fact. Violence defines the state. As Max Weber put the matter, the state is a group that successfully "claims the monopoly of the legitimate use of physical force within a given territory." But "legitimate" just means *legal*, not moral—especially as authorities determine what is legal and what is not.

We'll hire 80,000 IRS agents to coerce others to pay for foreign wars.

In other words, they threaten violence to export violence (or to pay those who would censor us). Morality is sacrificed to strategy.

Corruption. Though we don't talk about it enough, corruption is also part and parcel of government. It has degrees and kinds, of course. In some countries, officials take bribes. In America, they take campaign contributions. Political hierarchies select for sociopaths, because those who get on top are willing to use questionable means. Maybe a couple of politicians have integrity. But most have to auction it off to get anywhere. Otherwise, they have no power. And if voters think they can get something for free, they'll often look the other way when it comes to venality. In doing so, they become complicit.

We'll award billions to contractors and constituency groups but take a cut for our campaign coffers.

When power goes on the auction block, there is no morality among the sellers or the bidders.

Callousness. Does politics make people callous? We constantly hear, for example, that large European welfare states are more "compassionate" societies, even though the United States has an enormous welfare state of its own. But in both cases, extensive welfare states offer people an opportunity to outsource their compassion, not exercise it. That might not seem callous at first, but over time, centralized welfare engenders indifference. "I pay my taxes," they mutter as they hurry past the needy. Callousness also arrives when one views another as an ATM, that is, instead of giving of themselves. By posting their policy prescriptions online, they fancy they've done the work of being good. But redistribution isn't compassion. It's compulsion. And too often, welfare tempts recipients into dependency.

We'll write no checks to the U.S. Treasury ourselves but insist on compulsory taxes.

The most callous among us are often the most sanctimonious about who is to pay their "fair share." These are the watchwords of takers, not of givers or makers.

Monomania. Even though platforms change in the political winds, partisans tend to be monomaniacal. Notice how they're never wrong. Though technocrats are quick to trot out some lofty ideal, they almost always lack the knowledge required to bring about their *dirigisme*. When such policies fail or create perverse effects, they blame the other party or cry that their favored program isn't adequately funded.

We'll impose policies on you because they are the only way to fight the War on x or crisis y.

Lurking behind such words is the conceit of the *One True Way.*

Negligence. Centralists also imagine the state is somehow a good and rightful steward of resources. Yet the list of resources the government wastes constitutes a book unto itself. Governments incur debt larger than their productive output (GDP). Functionaries pay exorbitant sums to military contractors that no market would bear. The U.S. government is also the world's largest polluter. Its military alone pollutes more than 100 countries. Urban roads fall into disrepair as new highways get built in a congressman's wilderness district. Social Security's coffers are bare. Centralist systems create incentives to be negligent.

We'll punish you for waste, fraud, and abuse even though these are our modus operandi.

When accountability is missing, negligence prevails. The political class remains virtually unaccountable.

Casuistry. I don't need to explain how political elites spin narratives and twist truths. I need only point out that some of the biggest propagators of "disinformation" staff the U.S. government's Disinformation Board. That sorry subagency persists to this day despite the public sacrifice of Nina Jankowicz to a wiser mob that effectively called bullshit.

Journalists Ken Klippenstein and Lee Fang offered key takeaways in their 2022 reporting:

- Though DHS shuttered its controversial Disinformation Governance Board, a strategic document reveals the underlying work is ongoing.
- DHS plans to target inaccurate information on "the origins of the COVID-19 pandemic and the efficacy of COVID-19 vaccines, racial justice, U.S. withdrawal from Afghanistan, and the nature of U.S. support to Ukraine."

- Facebook created a special portal for DHS and
  government partners to report disinformation
  directly.[4]

For reasons that should be obvious, this sub-agency has
been called "The Ministry of Truth." Now, imagine the people
you distrust most take over the agency. Far from being
dedicated to tracking truth, it will be a weapon hijacked by the
very cynics and zealots you hate.

*We'll determine what misinformation is and become a
monopoly provider of misinformation.*

Disinformation and misinformation are newspeak for *that
with which I disagree.*

Some might argue that, though the Six Offenses are how
politics works, that's not how things *should* work. They
imagine that *if we could vote the right people into office,* those
angels would be able to overcome the perverse incentives of
politics.

Alas, there are no angels. Despite all the soaring words
about "our democracy," democracy is just another word for
politics. And contemporary politics brings out the worst in all
of us.

"Politics takes a continuum of possibilities and turns it into
a small group of discrete outcomes," write scholars Trevor
Burrus and Aaron Ross Powell, "often just two." The duo
continues:

Either this guy gets elected, or that guy does. Either a
given policy becomes law or it doesn't. As a result,
political choices matter greatly to those most affected.
An electoral loss is the loss of a possibility. These black
and white   choices   mean   politics   will   often

manufacture problems that previously didn't exist, such as the "problem" of whether we--as a community, as a nation--will teach children creation or evolution.[5]

Burrus and Powell don't stop there.

Politics like this is no better than arguments between rival sports fans, and often worse because politics is more morally charged. Most Americans find themselves committed to either the red team (Republicans) or the blue (Democrats) and those on the other team are not merely rivals, but represent much that is evil in the world. Politics often forces its participants into pointless internecine conflict, as they struggle with the other guy not over legitimate differences in policy opinion but in an apocalyptic battle between virtue and vice.[6]

The rival teams fail to realize that the difference between virtue and vice is the difference between practical morality and practical politics.

MISSION, MORALITY, AND MEANING

Whenever you aim at power's shibboleths, you will irritate partisans. Most people want to see their priors confirmed. When instead you offer them a taste of medicine, most will spit it right back at you.

The world has forgotten timeless truths.

Distracted by political spectacles and errant ideologies, a majority has replaced morality with politics. Political team sports prevail. Most have become too comfortable with expanding political power so long as it's for their team. Of course, these concerns are related and self-reinforcing. That's why, one way or another, we have to bring back *being good*—not to outsource that practice to distant capitals, but to cultivate moral practice in our communities and ourselves.

Even if it means shouting into the wind for a time, we must do everything possible to rediscover the ancient virtues that protect civilization. Without a deeper sense of mission, morality, mutualism, and meaning, no human system can thrive.

And, of course, we have to decentralize power. It's not merely that empires fall as night follows day. The growth of the managerial state continues to wreak havoc on innocent people who just want to pursue happiness. Some say civilizations rise and fall in natural cycles. They may be correct to the extent it is in our nature to embrace the tribal-coalitional turpitudes of politics. But suppose we can lock arms in solidarity around the idea of making a moral order together—including the Six Spheres—to layer atop a consent-based society.

We might just stop this vicious cycle and enjoy a renaissance.

3
THE GREAT AUTHORITARIAN ARMS RACE

Pick the target, freeze it, personalize it, and polarize it.
—Saul Alinsky, from *Rules for Radicals*[1]

THERE IS A QUOTE FLOATING AROUND, variously attributed to Lenin and to Marx, which enjoins authoritarians to:

Accuse your enemies of doing what you're doing.

Whether this was the work of Lenin, or a fortune-cookie writer in Akron, it doesn't matter. Powerful authorities are actively employing this tactic.

When the senile president gave his now-famous "Dark Brandon"[2] speech against a blood-red backdrop that authorities could have cribbed from a Leni Riefenstahl[3] film, it revealed as much about the machinations of the powerful as the depravity of their strategists.

"They promote authoritarian leaders," said the president, "and they fan the flames of political violence that are a threat to our personal rights, to the pursuit of justice, to the rule of law, to the very soul of this country."

Accuse your enemies of doing what you're doing.

Up to this point, authoritarians had been slowly boiling us lowly frogs. But the Politburo turned up the heat. The president continued:

"And now America must choose: to move forward or to move backwards? To build the future or obsess about the past? To be a nation of hope and unity and optimism, or a nation of fear, division, and of darkness?"

Click-click went the burner.

There is a sinister brilliance in calling for "unity" while simultaneously referring to almost half of the country as fascists. There is a glorious perversity in the psyop of calling voters extremists while directing the State Apparatus—that extraordinary fusion of corporate and state power—to censor speech and harass your political enemies. But the true genius lies in whipping half the country into such a frenzy that they are willing to let the Apparatus put the other half under thumb.

Who cares? They're just troglodytes. They are the Other. And it's being carried out in the name of *protecting our democracy.*

A STASI OF OUR OWN

The stage had been set in 2021 when the Department of Homeland Security (DHS) released an advisory memo warning that "domestic violent extremists (DVEs), including... anti-government/anti-authority violent extremists, will continue to pose a significant threat to our homeland."[4]

Speaking of anti-government/anti-authority extremists, let us not forget that one of the American Founders wrote that the "tree of liberty must be refreshed from time to time with the blood of patriots and tyrants."[45] Does it matter that today's anti-authoritarians are often peaceful people who want to express their skepticism of state power in a tweet?

To the DVE advisory memo, DHS Secretary Mayorkas adds that "DHS has renewed its commitment to work with our partners across every level of government, the private sector, and local communities to combat all forms of terrorism and targeted violence."[6]

DHS needn't conscript a Stasi. Volunteers have lined up to "work with" them. Nina "hide-a-little-lie" Jankovicz had been just another fangirl of the Apparatus before she was recruited to head up the Ministry of Truth, which, as we've seen, is still a thing.

Let us not forget that the FBI raids the homes of voters they don't like, and "works with" social media platforms such as Facebook and—at one time—Twitter to silence dissent and brand dissenters as extremists.

Click-click goes the burner.

When it comes to branding half of America extremists/fascists, Team Blue is positively credulous, sometimes frothing. That means they care as much about Team Red's rights as they do about those of the Uyghurs. Indeed, the deep state's efforts reveal more steps toward sino-forming America—up to and including a CBDC (Central Bank Digital Currency), a monetary panopticon that will roll out under the watchwords: *The innocent have nothing to fear.*

Those afraid of creeping authoritarianism coming from the Left might be inclined to look to the Right for electoral salvation. But increasingly, you will find that the other side will be motivated more by revenge than by the protection of any principles or American ideals. That means Team Red is likely to seize the Apparatus and turn it right back on Team Blue. Far from decrying such moves out of principle, Team Red will bask in all the Schadenfreude.

That is, until the pendulum swings back.

NEGATIVE SUM

The current configuration creates incentives for reprisals likely to swing back and forth until the Apparatus breaks down. And that could mean a civil war that pulls most of what is currently the "Indifferent Center" into picking a team.

So, the nation finds itself pulled into a game/theoretical construction that is unlikely to lead anywhere good or healthy. It's an arms race to see who can be more authoritarian.

The cleverest in the beltway will try to tell you otherwise, even those whose work you might have long admired. They have decided that the Evidence™ already demands you pick a team.

"Could we please retire the both-side-sist trope that both parties are captured by their radicals?" writes author Jonathan Rauch, who once wrote a book referring to radical social-justice advocates as "kindly inquisitors."

I'm reminded of the Nolan Chart, which, though not a perfect political typology, is more accurate than a spectrum that goes from left to right. Political scientist David Nolan added another axis—libertarian to authoritarian—designed to add an important vertical dimension to the sad old 2D left-right landscape. Libertarianism is at the top, and authoritarianism is at the bottom.

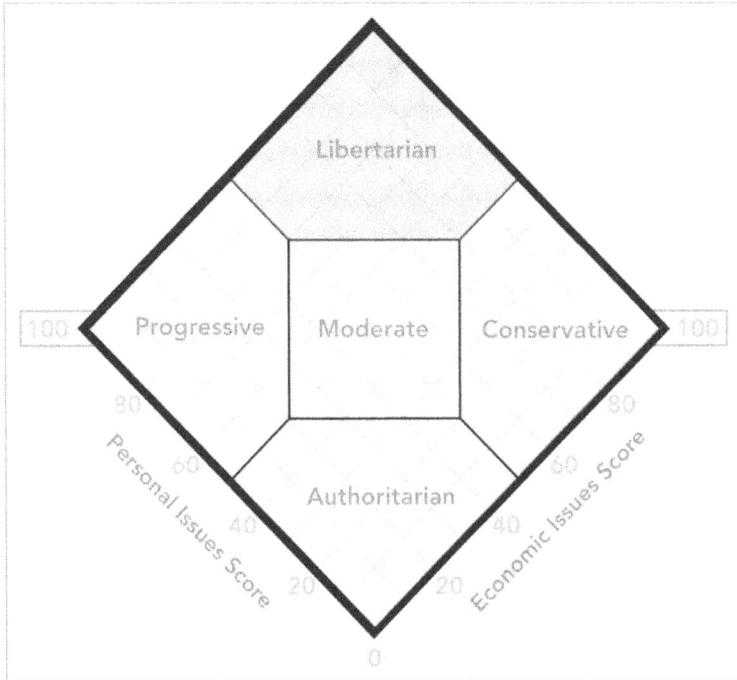

Unfortunately, today's incentives and culture have a gravity that pulls people down. That is, progressives, moderates, and conservatives are becoming more and more authoritarian by the day. If I'm correct, a balanced critique, far from being a fallacy, is a moral imperative.

Recall that in the early twentieth century, Redshirts and Brownshirts hated each other. But ideologically, they were kissing cousins.[7] It's not even clear that these groups are conscious of the irony. It's more that animus can turn people into what they claim to loathe. That's certainly happening today. Each side defines itself against its enemy and imagines it is on the side of the angels. They think of their tactics as necessary evils, and so, stepwise, embrace evil.

Click-click goes the burner.

Partisan intellectuals on either team will waggle their

fingers and warn us of "both-sides-ism," which they argue is a fallacy of false balance. It's as if they have special access to a cosmic scoreboard of authoritarianism. But in a matrix of incentives where both sides have strong incentives to engage in the more illiberal aspects of partisan tug-o-war, the partisans are just being selective in their outrage. They join in on the finger-pointing and *tu quoque*. You might find them scratching themselves, too, having lain down with dogs.

THE SUBMISSION INSTINCT

On a personal note, I am fully aware of the impulse to tolerate the growth of authoritarian power rooted in fear and animus. After 9/11, I was concerned, but I failed fully to appreciate the warnings about what kind of surveillance state measures such as the PATRIOT Act and, later, the spinning up of the new Department of Homeland Security (DHS), would mean for Americans' civil liberties. In hindsight, I can see that I had been overcome by fear and polarization. I, too, had picked a team.

Click-click went the burner.

Since then, far from sunsetting post-9/11 measures, subsequent administrations and legislatures have built on them to create what is now collectively known as the deep state. And in my relative silence, I might as well have been a cheerleader for its rise. Despite everything I knew about mission creep, I let myself worry too much about terrorism. Now, the deep state has turned its capabilities on ordinary citizens.

I understand that a few rare events have caused us all to raise our concerns about extremist violence against innocents, from church and synagogue killings to clashes between protestors resulting in deaths. To some degree, people accept that police powers must be applied to deal with such threats. But we must remain vigilant, for any police power that can be

turned on violent extremists can be turned on those merely *labeled* violent extremists.

Even though rare-but-scary things happen from time to time, including protests that burn out of control—whether May 29th, 2020 (BLM) or January 6, 2021 (MAGA)—events like these flow as much from ideological polarization as from evils endemic to ordinary Americans. The illiberal arms race builds on this. Both sides seek unity without pluralism, which is a kind of forced unity. It would be a grave mistake to let partisans pull the rest of us into something like this:

"It is the State which educates its citizens in civic virtue, gives them a consciousness of their mission, and welds them into unity."

A State run by whom? For whose idea of virtue? For what mission? And unity welded by what means? Both sides seem to have accepted Mussolini's words implicitly as they struggle to seize power and dominate the Other.

AFFECTIVE POLARIZATION

Citizens have always experienced some degree of "affective polarization" in politics, but columnist Stephanie Slade warns the phenomenon is getting worse. She writes:

Various studies have found that Americans today have significantly more negative feelings toward members of the other party than they did in decades past.

But partisan animosity suits the authoritarian elements on the left and right just fine. Their goal is power, and they have little patience for procedural niceties that interfere with its exercise. As history teaches, a base whipped up into fear and fury is ready to accept almost anything to ensure its own survival. Perhaps even the destruction of the institutions and ideals that make America distinctively itself.[8]

Slade is right, and she's got the data. Anyone who accuses her of "both-sides-ism" has his head where the sun don't shine.

So, no. Now is not the time to "retire the both-sides-ism trope," as Jonathan Rauch insist. It's time that an anti-authoritarian coalition turns against affective polarization and the impulse to pick a team. It's time we call out authoritarianism anywhere it rears its head. And we must do everything in our power to innovate so that there are exits from this crumbling, top-heavy conflict machine. God forbid any "side" wins this war. God forbid we descend into civil war at all, especially as the real authoritarians are waiting in the shadows as we continue to preoccupy ourselves with the spectacle of it all.

Click-click goes the burner.

4
LUXURY BELIEFS DEATH SPIRAL

The domestic life of most classes is relatively shabby, as compared with the éclat of that overt portion of their life that is carried on before the eyes of observers.
　—Thorstein Veblen[1]

IT USED to be that the wealthy elite distinguished themselves through so-called Veblen goods. Ostentatious displays like a big house or fancy car once sufficed to show you were a member of the upper crust. But times have changed. Today, to run among the elite, you have to show you care—with an emphasis on *show*.

If you believe social theorist Rob Henderson, today's elites hold *luxury beliefs*. Such beliefs cost little to hold and often benefit the holder by improving her reputation in the in-group. Therefore, she's likely to hold all manner of bizarre views. Most of these views will seem crazy to the plebs until they realize adopting them is a ticket to the cocktail party.

"The chief purpose of luxury beliefs," writes Henderson in *Quillette*, is to indicate evidence of the believer's social class and education."[2]

Henderson notices that the indirect costs of luxury beliefs are often borne by the poor and middle class, financially or in terms of direct consequences. But thanks to social media, telegraphing your virtue is cheaper than a carton of McDonald's French fries, despite costly effects on the rest of us.

BOTTOMLESS IDEALISM

"Starting salary for a teacher should be $125K and go up to $300-400K," writes a Facebook connection who wants desperately to preen and peacock his goodness.

Even though the average teacher salary in America ($65,090[3]) is higher than the mean personal income ($57,143) —and teachers work fewer than 190 days per year with hours similar to other workers[4]—the well-to-do can afford to think that starting teachers ought to make mad money. In most states, though, teacher salaries are funded by sales taxes or property taxes, which fall disproportionately on the poor and middle classes.

"No Human Is Illegal," read millions of yard signs in wealthy enclaves.

SCIENCE IS REAL
BLACK LIVES MATTER
NO HUMAN IS ILLEGAL
LOVE IS LOVE
WOMEN'S RIGHTS
ARE HUMAN RIGHTS
KINDNESS IS EVERYTHING

But, as the denizens of Martha's Vineyard will tell you, it's cheap to put up a yard sign. It's far more costly to take care of real people who turn up in your community with nothing.

Forty-four hours after Florida Governor Ron Desantis's stunt to fly fifty Venezuelans to the sanctuary island, Martha's Vineyard's elites (median income $82,857) sent the immigrants packing. It was purportedly because those elites lacked the "infrastructure" to help. Of course, the people of Brownsville, Texas (median income $40,924) can relate.

Even if one thinks, as I do, that we can set up policies that will do more to welcome and place immigrants, there is no doubt that the current immigration regime is a mess. In any case, those fifty poor Venezuelans will almost certainly end up in poorer areas with strained infrastructures.

Some humans are illegal, apparently.

"This idea that you spend money on an education as a cover charge to a career should be laughed out of the room," tweets one virtuous soul cheering on the executive's constitutionally spurious debt-forgiveness plan. Instead, this Tweeter writes, education should, "form and complete them as people."[5]

The idea here is that in Utopia, higher education should be available to everyone for "free." It's one thing to hold such views. It's quite another to figure out how to pay for it. Never mind that the cost of autodidacticism, educating oneself, is already close to zero.

LUXURY BELIEFS ARE CHEAP FOR NOW

The problem with luxury beliefs is that they're not just for the rich anymore. These beliefs are trickling down to everyone at a steep discount as non-elites try to emulate elites.

The problem with luxury-belief emulation is people tend

to vote their beliefs, especially when there is no direct cost to doing so. But that means aggregate costs balloon, and those costs get shifted to taxpayers or added to the Treasury's tab.

When most people read that the U.S. debt-to-G.D.P. ratio is more than 130 percent, their eyes glaze over. But to put this into perspective, only three developed countries—Greece, Lebanon, and Japan—have higher ratios. And there is growing concern any one of these countries could start a sovereign-debt contagion, particularly in a world where there is about $300 trillion in debt floating around but only $100 trillion in economic output per year.

POOR FOLKS' TRUTHS

I don't know whether Rob Henderson would approve, but I'd like to propose a corollary to the concept of luxury beliefs: poor folks' truths. Where luxury beliefs are cheap to hold but expensive overall, poor folks' truths might be socially costly to hold, but they better track reality, including any indirect consequences to the poor and middle class.

BELIEF MATRIX		
Socially costly to hold	Batshit Crazy	Poor Folks' Truths
Socially acceptable to hold	Luxury Beliefs	Tried and True Truths
	Dubious or costly in reality	True or necessary in reality

One major poor folks' truth is an idea that runs counter to all the luxury beliefs currently swirling around out there: austerity. Short of any major institutional change, the U.S. federal government has reached the stage where it must stop spending increases or risk calamity. Unprecedented debts loom as dark storm clouds over the republic, but no one wants to talk about it. Austerity ain't sexy. It certainly doesn't make you friends at cocktail parties.

Imagine you have a friend who makes $40,000 per year in salary after taxes but also carries $300,000 in various debts. He would have a hard time ever paying down his debt, and it's not clear that any rational person would loan money to him again. If he could set aside $500 per month to pay debts at 6 percent interest, it would take him 636 months to pay it all off. That's 53 years. Now, the U.S. Federal Government, though analogous, operates at a scale that is as complicated as it is humongous. The difference is that our government doesn't include what would be the parallel $500 per month to pay down its debt. So, if the federal government were this "friend," you might want to offer a socially costly poor folks' truth: *stop spending or default.*

THE DEATH SPIRAL

Every time parties change power, the winners want to spend, spend, spend to reestablish the power they lost when out of office. Politicians do this by greasing the palms of their favored constituencies and special interests. We used to call that corruption. These days we just call it politics, as we have become inured to the idea that the government has two departments: Do Something and Gimme Gimme. Otherwise, it's just another day for power brokers to indulge those enlightened few who are happy to hold all manner of nutty beliefs, even though they threaten any number of devastating socioeconomic scenarios. Debt heaps upon debt. Inflation lingers.

For those rare politicians with a conscience, the bind looks like this: Voters, even those who have moved right, still think the role of government is to help people. But decades of government "assistance" have gotten us into this sorry state, as more than 60 percent of federal outlays are for healthcare and welfare transfers. Free-market fundamentalists have always argued that the only way for a people to get wealthy is to create wealth in a system of private property, undistorted prices, profit-or-loss, and sound money.

There is no other way. But most voters don't realize this.

To repeat, most think the role of government is to *help people*, especially in hard times. According to the left-leaning Center for American Progress, a 2021 poll indicates that "American voters want the government to play a strong role in securing basic living standards for all people."[6] Assuming this poll is valid, voters will expect more help as matters worsen. If politicians offer more largess, they risk default, or the Federal Reserve will have to print more money. Printing money causes inflation, and that's just as painful, as a new generation is learning.

If politicians were to cut government spending, exactly what they need to do, voters would likely turn on them. If politicians don't cut much of anything, Americans will stay mired in recession, or worse, and turn on them anyway.

The only way the authorities can get us out of this mess is to be straight with voters. Instead of lying and spending, politicians must become standard-bearers of values most people have forgotten: working hard, saving, creating value, and looking out for your neighbor. And they will have to do so at the risk of losing power.

A question remains.

Short of welcoming the brutal circumstances that would force everyone to experience the immediate pain of decades-long cost shifting and debt spending, how can we reduce the social costs of sharing poor folks' truths? And how can we raise the social costs of luxury beliefs? I wish I had an easy answer.

If we don't figure it out, we're all going to suffer mightily— except, that is, the elite. They'll be in the best position to absorb the costs of any coming crisis. Indeed, they will be well positioned to continue thriving on a vampiric system that feasts on the lifeblood of the poor and middle class.

5

THE DEEP STATE IS BREAKING DOWN

You can't handle the truth.
  —Col. Jessup, from A Few Good Men[1]

SINCE THE FRANK CHURCH COMMITTEE investigations of the 1970s, the deep state's information-control structure remains functional. The FBI, CIA, and more recently the DHS and other agencies, have been shaping the narrative and replacing news with information warfare for decades. Americans' minds are the battlespace. But as media continue to decentralize, the deep state is starting to lose control.

Now that a new Church-style investigation is in the offing, one wonders if it'll do any more good than the last one. The overall warping of our collective intelligence has been helped by countless stories on TV and in movies portraying our alphabet-soup agencies as heroes, despite real-world mission creep and deep corruption. Nicolas Schou details this whitewashing phenomenon in his 2016 article[2] and related book, *Spooks*:

In 1996, the CIA hired one of its veteran clandestine officers, Chase Brandon, to work directly with Hollywood studios and production companies to upgrade its image. "We've always been portrayed erroneously as evil and Machiavellian," Brandon later told *The Guardian*. "It took us a long time to support projects that portray us in the light we want to be seen in."

But as revelations surrounding NSA spying on American citizens surfaced due to the Edward Snowden leaks, it has become clearer that deep-state players are, indeed, Machiavellian. Their objective is to maintain social coherence around their power. Their mantra is *Exitus acta probat*, the ends justify the means. Along with long-standing corruption, partisan contagions now infect their ranks—with agencies being more thoroughly politicized and weaponized, and turned on ordinary Americans.[3]

REVEALING THE ROT

Recent work by indie journalists, such as those working on the Twitter files[4] and others that reveal details of various leaked DHS documents,[5] offer proof of deep-state actors willing to pull out all the extralegal stops. The efforts are meant to keep the herds timid and credulous—with the deep state firmly in control. The blue-check Twitterati's response to suspicions had been "Conspiracy theorists!" right up until the evidence dropped, whereupon it was a "Nothingburger!"

Groupthink meets gaslighting.

But what happened to journalism as a check on power? Armies of J-school grads had gone from modeling themselves after Woodward and Bernstein, questioning authority, to modeling themselves after Pravda—with a dash of Judith Butler thrown in for good measure. Newspapers of record were captured by activists. Readers craved team sports over truth and the J-school activists served it up.

The proverbial march through the institutions continued in the deep state, as well, until corporate media crawled into bed with the G-men. What monstrosities nurse in Langley and Quantico?

Mainstream journalism went from speaking truth to power to shouting power over truth. This shift put several veteran truth-seekers in the unpleasant position of admitting that Donald Trump was right, at least in part: The 2020 election had been "stolen," at least in the sense that the U.S. government actively interfered. Not Russians, Americans (see receipts in the box below). But a few independent reporters, many of whom are on the dissident left, revealed a Bizarro world of allegations against the Biden family's corruption in China and Ukraine. "Bizarro" because Americans had spent years listening to hollow accusations of Russian collusion, which had all along been a contrivance of the DNC in collaboration with the FBI. This scheme included the likes of former FBI attorney Jim Baker,[6] who, journalist Bari Weiss figured out, was the fox guarding Twitter's henhouse.[7]

Whether and to what extent unconstitutional actions by the deep state are *justifiable* has now become a partisan shuttlecock among the Twitterati. However, this is a significant sea change from a people who once understood themselves as united in principles of accountable authority. For far too long, deep-state actors such as FBI agent Elvis Chan[8] had been able to evade accountability and shape narratives to reinforce Americans' faith in the Church of State.

The mainstream media are now cheerleaders in such efforts, confusing partisanship with patriotism. Worse still, agents and spooks have been able to infiltrate all the major social media companies by paying or pressuring proxies to disappear truth-tellers and send dissent down the memory hole.

RECENT EXAMPLES OF DEEP STATE VIOLATIONS

COVID

Notable people censored at the behest of the U.S. government include Harvard epidemiologist Martin Kuldorff, journalist Alex Berenson,[9] and Stanford economist Jay Bhattacharya.[10]

Head of the National Institutes of Health (NIH), Francis Collins, along with the head of NIAID, the infectious disease sub-agency, Anthony Fauci put AIER in its crosshairs for hosting the Great Barrington Declaration. Thanks to a FOIA request, we now know Collins wrote, "there needs to be a quick and devastating published takedown of its premises."[11] As of this writing, more evidence of censorship pressure from the NIH and the CDC is coming to light.

Innumerable citizens were deplatformed for either questioning the "natural origins" theory of COVID or asking questions about the lab-leak theory. Since this mass censorship, a number of mainstream journalists began openly questioning the theory of natural origins, prompting social media companies to relax their censorship of ordinary users.

After sternly worded letters from the likes of Senator Elizabeth Warren (D-MA) and Congressman Adam Schiff (D-CA), Amazon removed books that these and other state agents referred to as "misinformation."[12]

The U.S. government even pressured the Canadian government to censor and freeze the accounts of protestors in Ottawa who had been part of the Freedom Convoy, a group of truckers opposing vaccine mandates, passports, and other travel restrictions.

2016 Election

The FBI, in collusion with the Clinton campaign and the Democratic National Committee, assisted in propagating the now-discredited Russian-interference narrative, with one agent going so far as to claim (falsely) that the original source of the Russia accusation had been the DOJ. Such accusations prompted the FBI to investigate the newly-elected President Trump, based solely on rumor and "evidence" associated with the fraudulent Steele dossier.

Recovered texts also revealed that rogue agents were bent on taking down the newly-elected president Trump: "He's not ever going to become president, right? Right?!"[13] to which the other agent replied, "No, No he's not. We'll stop it." The agents had attempted to delete these texts, but forensic teams located them.

A group (Hamilton 68) of former spooks and G-men associated with an eely organization known as The Alliance for Securing Democracy, make multiple requests to take down

"Russian bots'" Twitter accounts, which turned out to be accounts of ordinary Americans.

Whistleblowers

According to Congressional Republicans, fourteen FBI whistleblowers came forward to accuse the Bureau of a "systemic culture of unaccountability," full of "rampant corruption, manipulation, and abuse."[14]

The accusers say the FBI is: artificially inflating statistics about domestic violent extremism in the nation; abusing its counterterrorism authority to investigate parents who spoke at school-board meetings; abusing its foreign intelligence authority to spy on American citizens, including people associated with the campaign of President Trump in 2016; clearing the Bureau of employees who dissent from its politicized agenda.

2020 Election

The FBI also pressured companies to censor the *New York Post*'s reporting on the Hunter Biden laptop, justifying the pressure due to what the Bureau termed a so-called "hack and leak" operation.[15] Yet the FBI had been in possession of the Biden laptop *for almost a year* and could vouch for its existence. The agency did not do so. Instead, agents told social-media companies it was likely the work of "Russians"—a psyop designed to elicit compliance, making the suppression a crime of election interference rivaling Watergate.

Fifty former national-security-state operatives, including

former CIA director John Brennan, signed a letter claiming that the infamous Hunter Biden laptop was "Russia trying to influence how Americans vote in this election, and we believe strongly that Americans need to be aware of this."[16]

As with the attempted kidnapping of Governor Gretchen Whitmer,[17] many observers wonder whether the FBI was involved in planning or encouraging January 6th protestors to breach the Capitol. If true, the psyop narrative would be designed to frame Trump voters as "insurrectionists," and, especially, Trump for directing the coup.

The Atlantic Council, staffed by seven former CIA heads and funded by the Ukrainian energy company Burisma (yes, the Burisma implicated in the laptop scandal), partnered with Facebook and the DHS to monitor "election misinformation." According to sources familiar with the matter, 22 million tweets were labeled "misinformation" on Twitter, with a *unanimous* partisan bias.[18]

Secretary of State, Anthony Blinken, while on President Biden's campaign staff, concocted the idea of having 50 national security state-affiliated people sign a letter to the effect that the Hunter Biden laptop story had all the hallmarks of "Russian" disinformation. Then CIA Director, Mike Morell, when asked why he was complicit in the Fifty's election interference letter, replied he wanted to, "help Vice President Biden... because I wanted him to win the election."[19]

Disinformation

According to documents leaked to *The Intercept*, the DHS

doggedly pursued the shaping of national narratives, despite the sudden dismantling of the Disinformation Governance Board after popular backlash. DHS officials pledged to target "inaccurate information" on a wide range of topics, including "the origins of the COVID-19 pandemic and the efficacy of COVID-19 vaccines, racial justice, U.S. withdrawal from Afghanistan, and the nature of U.S. support to Ukraine."[20]

The National Science Foundation (NSF) spent $38.8 million on government grants and contracts to combat "misinformation" since the start of the Biden administration.[21] "Misinformation" is information that works against the deep state's agenda. The upshot is: You are being compelled to pay for your censors.

DEAD PRESIDENTS

In 2022, after the Biden Administration released an incomplete trove of files associated with the JFK assassination, more investigators are coming around to the view that the CIA was responsible for killing the thirty-fifth president.[22] The recent trove helps to draw a closer connection between Lee Harvey Oswald and the CIA. Even though all of the documents were required, by law, to have been released by 2017, every president since the 1992 law's passage has fought to keep the remaining documents sealed. What on earth would prompt five different presidents to cover it up?

One shudders.

The thought that the deep state has been far more *in control* for much longer than most of us imagine is deeply disturbing. Not only does the national-security state function as a mafia, but some commenters also suspect that organized crime and the deep state became entangled a long time ago.[23]

The minds of "conspiracy theorists" get set alight. As they should. Ironic that the deep state popularized the term *conspiracy theory* to dispel questions beyond the Warren Commission's report. In other words, the accusation was a psyop from the start, designed to make investigators look crazy. Subsequently, though, critics chipped away at the official narrative, so much so that by 1966 popular faith in the Warren report was already shaken. The government's story seemed *too* simple, pimpled and bleeding with Occam's Razor burn.

BREAKDOWN

The silver lining is that we are witnessing the breakdown of the deep state, which is part of what social theorist Jordan Hall calls the Blue Church:

The abstract is this: the Blue Church is a kind of narrative/ideology control structure that is a natural result of mass media. It is an evolved (rather than designed) function that has come over the past half-century to be deeply connected with the Democratic political "Establishment" and lightly connected with the "deep state" to form an effective political and dominant cultural force in the United States.[24]

Such cultural dominance means the deep state has had to multiply its tendrils to infiltrate all the new vectors of media influence:

The key insight for this post is that as an audience we are coherent. As a mass, we transform from millions of diverse individuals into one, relatively simple, group. So long as we can be maintained in this coherence, we present something that can be managed.

This is the formal core of the Blue Church: it solves the problem of 20th Century social complexity through the use of mass media to generate manageable social coherence.[25]

But in the twenty-first century, something changed.

The Internet brought decentralization and the rise of digital insurgencies, forces that—though sometimes disorienting—changed the dynamic. The medium, following social theorist Marshall McLuhan, is still the message. Or as former CIA analyst Martin Gurri writes: "McLuhan was among the first to grasp that the *structure* of information is far more determinative than the *content*." [26](My emphasis.) For better or worse, then, authorities' desire to fashion social coherence is becoming increasingly difficult. Though Internet usage has consolidated around big social media companies, decentralization continues to restructure information in ways that allow digital insurgencies to emerge.

Anti-authoritarians don't want social coherence at the expense of the truth. We want the truth. Will the market provide a suitable medium? Currently, we're looking for salvation from politicians and billionaires. We have to do better.

No one can confirm whether Kennedy, in the wake of the Bay of Pigs fiasco, said he wished to "splinter the C.I.A. in a thousand pieces and scatter it to the winds." But such threats would not be taken as idle by powerful elites inside the agency, including those with ties with international criminal syndicates. With Kennedy out of the picture, they could act with relative impunity. And for decades after the assassination, they did.

These days when Senators Schumer and McConnell meet behind closed doors to drop an Omnibus slush fund bill, it's not very different from the meeting of the "five families." The powerful are negotiating ways to extort more from Americans. It's no accident that the FBI makes out like a bandit.[27]

But as the Internet continues, in fits and starts, to decentralize, anonymize, and integrate cryptography, the deep state's control structures could continue to founder.

We can imagine more intrepid reporters such as Ryan Grim, Matt Taibbi, Lee Fang, Whitney Webb, Glenn Greenwald, and Bari Weiss continuing to dig, learn, and tell the truth about the lengths to which deep-state actors will go to shape national narratives.

We can also imagine a thousand more citizen journalists acting as digital insurgents.

We can imagine a decentralized, open-source version of Wikileaks that allows anyone to upload whistleblower documents from anywhere onto an immutable blockchain. (Psst, *hey blockchain developers*—stop futzing about with goofy projects like NFTs.)

We can imagine truth-tracking systems built similarly to betting markets.

We can imagine other countries, eager to see an empire fall, decouple from America's dollar hegemony. If they do, it's unclear how the federal government will continue to fund the encroachment of these illiberal agencies in our information commons. The U.S. government, after all, is broke.

The aggregate effect of such measures will be the continued

breakdown of deep-state control structures. For better or worse, this process seems to be underway. Indeed, we see not a sudden turn by deep-state actors to self-serving extralegal agendas; they've always been self-serving. What we see is that *we* can finally see it—a glimpse, at least.

The only remaining question is whether we can stomach what we'll find once it all falls down.

PART TWO
ALTERNATIVES

6

DON'T MESS WITH OUR ROOTS

But the special function of certain Newspeak words, of which OLDTHINK was one, was not so much to express meanings as to destroy them.
—George Orwell, from *1984*

WHEN TWO CLIMATE-CHANGE activists went into a London museum and tossed tomato soup all over Van Gogh's *Sunflowers*, they didn't do their movement any favors. The act struck most people as petty terrorism, like something from the Cultural Revolution. One suspects this is just the sort of antics that have driven thinkers such as traditionalist Paul Kingsnorth away from the environmental movement. (More on him later.)

Recall that the Chinese Red Guard had been encouraged to destroy the Four Olds: Old Ideas, Old Culture, Old Customs, and Old Habits. Mao had prompted the Red Guard student movement to shore up Chinese Communism, which, at the time, the party viewed as the end of history. The Red

Guard wanted to destroy anything that might remind people of society before Mao. So they destroyed art, burned books, and toppled statues.

We are witnessing the return of the Red Guard. But this time, the call for the destruction of the Four Olds issues not from the CCP, but rather from Western universities. It's no secret that the academy is the beating heart of radical social-justice ideology, which, today, extends its tendrils into corporations, primary schools, athletics programs, and modern media.

As György Lukács and other European intellectuals sympathetic to Marx understood, to reprogram a people, you have to destroy their roots. Where Lukács failed, Mao succeeded. By cutting away China's roots, the communist dictator could usher in subsequent eras of totalitarian control. I call these roots the *substrata* because, as we will see, our psychosocial development is *layered*. We derive a significant portion of our self-concept from these layers of rootedness. But radical social-justice activists view healthy self-concept as a demonic force to be exorcised, perhaps a weed to be plucked from a utopian garden. To rid people of healthy self-concept, radical social-justice activists attack any sources of meaning that challenge their doctrine.

Much of the so-called "meaning crisis" comes from the mass deployment of radical social-justice mind viruses. The result has been an insidious mob psychology that continues to spread like a contagion. The layers of humanity upon which we understand ourselves and derive meaning can resist change, but radical social-justice activists want to obliterate all resistance. It matters not that such changes can leave people sick, poor, depressed, or physically altered. To make the postmodern omelet, you have to break a few eggs.

SUBSTRATA: LIBERALISM AND TRADITIONALISM

Educational entrepreneur Michael Strong refers to academia as "The World's Leading Social Problem."[1] To make his case, Strong points out that nineteenth-century liberals believed in two basic ideas:

- An economic system consisting of property rights, rule of law, and freedom of contract led to "the wealth of nations" and was a sound foundation for peace between nations.
- Personal virtues such as hard work, perseverance, ingenuity, initiative, self-discipline, personal responsibility, good manners, and wholesome living could put any individual on the path to a life in which he or she could become "healthy, wealthy, and wise."

Strong says these two basic points had been mainstream thinking in the United States and Britain. But, "for the next hundred years, most of the intellectual and pedagogical activity of university professors in the humanities and social sciences was dedicated to undermining respect for those ideas."

Such undermining persists to this day.

Academics embraced various flavors of socialism, and many continue to do so. Whether Maoists, Marxists, or mendicants of subtler shades of radical social justice, their modus operandi is to undermine liberalism. As critical race theorists Delgado and Stefancic write:

> Unlike traditional civil rights, which embraces incrementalism and step-by-step progress, critical theory questions the very foundations of the liberal order, including equality theory, legal reasoning, Enlightenment rationalism, and neutral principles of constitutional law. [2]

These "foundations" are the substrata—part of our American roots. They are also the adopted roots of those around the world who value the blessings of liberty.

But activists can read between the lines. Step One is to *question* those foundations. Step Two is to *dismantle* them. Those rushing to strike at the roots of the liberal order know full well that behind the veneer of concern for marginalized groups lies a will to power. Yet they will be the first to refer to everyone they loathe as fascists.

Some argue that true *liberalism*—a doctrine that holds that people ought to live in peace, pluralism, and freedom under the rule of law—is wholly at odds with traditional values. Even some self-styled classical liberals argue that there's nothing to see here when it comes to radical social justice. Others, like classical liberal writer Aaron Ross Powell, have decided to pick a partisan team.

"We can work ourselves into a moral panic about left-wing wokeism," writes Powell, "but the GOP has become the party of American fascism, and that's a good deal more of a problem than getting yelled at by Millennials and Gen Zers for refusing to use someone's preferred pronouns."

Yes, this is the same Aaron Ross Powell who, a decade before, wrote so stirringly about what politics does to us all. [3]

I consider Powell a friend and have worked with him. But like many intellectuals who have done too many tours of duty in the Beltway, I worry that he has been captured and suffers from a kind of Stockholm Syndrome. As a post-enlightenment liberal, I wish Powell and others like him would take care not to try to sever the connection among the strata. That would be a terrible mistake. At best, it would mean turning a blind eye to the destructive nature of radical social justice. At worst, it would mean people who claim to cherish freedom are hacking at its roots.

None of this is to argue for right-wing authoritarianism. As one committed to the Founders' Project, I recognize that we must be steadfast in our both-sides-ism. I argue, we are currently navigating between the Scylla of radical social-justice and the Charybdis of so-called National Conservatism. Yet true liberalism also leaves room for those with progressive and conservative values to self-determine within a broader liberal framework.

Of course, liberals and traditionalists will clash from time to time. But as the petty terrorists of radical social justice continue their march of vandalism through the institutions— sometimes literally, as in the BLM damage of 2020—many liberals, traditionalists, and moderate progressives will find a common cause in pushing back. Indeed, as a techno-optimist with an anarchist streak, I never thought I'd find myself nodding along with Paul Kingsnorth, a reformed climate activist turned Orthodox Christian, who occasionally flings holy water at the Technium.

Kingsnorth writes:

Back in America—now ground-zero for the abolition of biology—thousands of girls are undergoing double mastectomies, and teenage boys are being given "puberty-blocking" drugs designed to chemically castrate rapists. Eleven-year-old girls are taught that "if you feel uncomfortable in your body, it means you are transgender"—which may explain why, in some classrooms, a quarter of the children identify as precisely that. The concept of "trans kids'—a notion that would have been inconceivably baffling to most people even a few years back, and for many still is—is now being pushed so hard that it starts to look less like the liberation of an oppressed minority than an agenda to reprogramme society with an entirely new conception of the human body—and thus of nature itself. (Passage lightly edited for style.)[4]

Radical social-justice activists are destroying the biological substrate, much like American iconoclasts are toppling statues of Thomas Jefferson—symbols of our liberal substrate.

Attempts to dismantle our shared historical substrate are one thing. It would be quite another to mess with the family. But Lily Sánchez, writing in *Current Affairs*,[5] says hold my beer: The family must be abolished, which means a "breaking open of the family to free and unleash what's good in it and to generalize that into the social body as a whole. To make the necessary forms of care available to everyone unconditionally."

See? To unleash what is good about the family, you have to destroy the family; just as to unleash what is good about being a girl, you have to destroy the very concept of a girl as well as girls' and boys' bodies. To make a postmodern omelet... According to radical social-justice activists, these substrata are merely contingent. Chesterton's useless old fences stand in the way of progress.

Now, what if I told you that this urge to destroy the substrata follows a historical pattern?

THE INTEGRAL HEURISTIC

In Spiral Dynamics[6]—a framework of psychosocial values development first advanced by psychologist Clare Graves—the basic idea is that individuals and groups change over time according to certain *life conditions*. While some readers will prefer alternative stage theories, such as those of Harvard psychologist Robert Kegan, all such theories share a common idea. Human psychosocial development changes according to levels of complexity.

Because it's most familiar to me, I'll use the Spiral Dynamics framework as a heuristic, along with a sketch of social complexity through time. You'll notice that a color change indicates a new stage. As each stage is connected to a prior stage, picture in your mind the spiral starting at Beige and spiraling upward, even as you read the chart from up to down. The colors are useful, particularly as references to the associated values.

On the right side of the chart, you'll notice we begin with low complexity. But as societies develop through time, the complexity increases. That is, humans arrange themselves and their rules according to their need to process information and maintain coherence. When they can no longer maintain said coherence, they evolve along with the values that shore up the corresponding structures.

SPIRAL DYNAMICS OVERVIEW + COMPLEXITY	
Values Development	**Complexity Through Time**
TIER ONE	
1. <u>Beige</u> Survival instincts, reflexes	<u>Low</u> Helpless human
2. <u>Purple</u> Animist, mystical, tribal	<u>Low</u> Hunter/Gatherer Tribes
3. <u>Red</u> Egocentric, dominating	<u>Low/Medium</u> Warring Clans
4. <u>Blue</u> Authority, tradition, hierarchic	<u>Medium</u> Great Kingdoms/Empires
5. <u>Orange</u> Scientific, strategic, commercial	<u>Medium/High</u> Liberal Republics
6. <u>Green</u> Sensitive, relativistic, egalitarian	<u>Medium/High</u> Social Democracies
TIER TWO	
7. <u>Yellow</u> Systemic, agentic, emergent	<u>High</u> Decentralized, Polycentric Orders
8. <u>Turquoise</u> Holistic, receptive, harmonious	<u>High</u> Holonic Orders

According to this model, as civilizations become more complex, people develop different values and modes of cognition. Development has been intermittent and heterogeneous. Still, a few have managed to ascend to Tier Two. Most, though, linger somewhere in Tier One. And when they do, they tend to cling to a monolithic value system. They find the others disorienting.

Practitioners of this heuristic emphasize that, instead of wars among value systems, people can learn to *transcend* and *include* the values of prior levels, but this usually happens with Yellow. So, for example, a highly rational scientist (Orange) might eschew the beliefs of religious orthodoxy that hold sway in the prior stage (Blue). But the scientist might eventually come to see that there are features of Blue worth preserving, such as respect for elders or guarding certain traditions. In other words, you can *transcend* Blue traditionalism to see the world through the Orange lens of enlightenment liberalism—but also *include* Blue's healthier values.

Integral practitioners such as Ken Wilber have noted the excesses of the Green stage—with its emphasis on hyperrelativism and the rejection of human nature, rationality, and truth. Wilber worries Green can be a psychosocial ditch. He observes that "Mean Green" represents the values of a new Cultural Revolution. Radical social justice, according to Wilber, is an unhealthy expression of Green that militates against the prior substrata, whereas healthy development requires synthesizing prior values, not going to partisan war with them. For example, Mean Greens talk about tolerance but only with respect to marginalized groups. They spurn other values. "Inclusion," far from calling on us to integrate diverse worldviews, is but shop talk for the intersectional props in Green victimhood narratives.

I am sympathetic to the idea that, in psychosocial development, we can retain healthy expressions of prior stages. For example, when I go home to my native North Carolina, I find myself saying ma'am and sir, despite my letters and laurels. Mean Greens would view this as some abhorrent reinforcement of dangerous gender stereotypes designed to erase the existence of "genderqueers" and "two-spirits." For example, writes thought-police officer Brooklyn Reece:

The server comes up to you and brings you and your friend cups of iced water. When they place the glass in front of you, they chirp, "Here you go, ma'am!"

A wave of tension and self-consciousness sweeps through you. You consider the situation. Was it the long hair? The earrings? The lipstick? Which feminine-stereotyped accessory gave your server the right to assume your gender identity? When did they ever ask you your pronouns?[7]

Only such a bizarre neopuritan ideology would prompt one to attack ma'am and sir as OLDTHINK. It must be difficult and frustrating to decouple oneself from humanity's culturally and biologically evolved layers. Perhaps the tribal proclivities of the Purple stage, mingled with the dominating urges of Red, unconsciously prompt Reece to *dismantle* and *destroy* rather than transcend and include.

Still, instead of going to civil war against these zealous Greens, is there a way to help them out of their ditch? After all, once they learn to transcend and include, most Greens aren't Green anymore.

RETURN OF THE KINGSNORTH

As quickly as I found myself nodding along with Paul Kingsnorth on protecting our roots, I turned to find him brandishing a machete next to mine.

First, Kingsnorth writes glowingly of illiberal conservative Patrick Deneen who routinely dances two-steps between the "liberalism" of technocratic progressives and the original liberalism of the American Founders. It's no wonder then that Kingsnorth has this assessment of liberalism:

The ideology of liberalism has, since it emerged from the Enlightenment, claimed to liberate the individual from oppression. In practice it has manifested as the process of breaking all borders, limits and structures: of bringing down walls. The societies we have built around this way of seeing claim freedom for the individual from society itself, and proffer a radical notion of human nature. Rather than seeing humans as hefted creatures, rooted in time and place, liberalism offered a new conception: detached, sovereign personhood. Humans were now "rights-bearing individuals who could fashion and pursue for themselves their own version of the good life."[8]

Did I say liberals and traditionalists will clash? Christ, straw is everywhere! I hope a loved one was there to sweep and check Kingsnorth's pulse after he so thoroughly and violently thwacked that poor fellow.

While Kingsnorth rightly notes that radical social-justice types are hacking away at the roots of human nature, he turns around and takes a stab at our *shared* roots (Kingsnorth is a Brit). Integral thinkers won't be surprised. Even the best first-tier thinkers have difficulty *transcending and including*. As Kingsnorth has become a valiant knight in Blue's shrinking kingdom, he sometimes retreats too far into the cramped recesses of that value system.

But not always.

Kingsnorth writes admiringly of Simone Weil's heterodox thinking here:

> Her attachment was to the eternal things, and she could never be boxed in. She wrote in praise of God, tradition, roots, peoples and culture; but also of justice, freedom of speech and thought, honour and equality. She could be equally scathing about fascism, communism, established religion, liberal elites, capitalism and mass education.[9]

Kingsnorth should not box himself in, either. After all, free speech is a liberal value. And we liberals can be just as scathing about fascism and communism, to the point that we define ourselves as the opposite of these. Further, original liberalism doesn't seek to break "all borders, limits, and structures." Instead, liberalism recommends porous borders that let people organize themselves within communities of peaceful pluralism. As Alexis de Tocqueville wrote:

> Wherever, at the head of a new undertaking, you see in France the government, and in England, a great lord, count on seeing in the United States, an association.[10]

Sadly, progressive technocrats destroyed most of America's great associations in the twentieth century. But technocrats don't like true liberalism, either. Indeed, they share the same contempt for associations that Lily Sánchez has for the family. In any case, I invite Kingsnorth to witness the beauty that Tocqueville saw when America *lived* its liberalism.

Despite Kingsnorth's strawman, liberalism doesn't require a "detached, sovereign personhood." Our doctrine acknowledges human interdependency while respecting individuals as something other than the chattel of the church, state, or ruling class. Liberalism doesn't seek freedom "from society itself." Instead, liberals know that the ties that bind a community are stronger when woven by people who associate freely, as opposed to when zealots have to shame, conquer, and convert them.

Liberalism, at least in its original form, seeks harmony with the natural order. Properly conceived, the doctrine is not about tearing anything down except arbitrary barriers that would otherwise prevent more organic forms of organization from emerging via peaceful human choices.

Paul Kingsnorth *chose* to convert to Orthodox Christianity. Surely his faith is bolstered by that choice, as opposed to the paltry faith one might find when baptism seems a better idea than torture. The difference is one of *agency*, which liberalism offers as a central value. I suspect that if God exists, God prefers us to *choose* moral acts rather than having goons compel us.

While liberalism carves out space for different traditions, with peaceability as the limiting principle, the reverse isn't always true. Kingsnorth should therefore take another look at liberalism. He might find some roots there. Indeed, he might even find *traditionalist* roots in liberalism, as Edmund Burke did. As Daniel Klein and Dominic Pino explain:

"Conservative liberalism" is a suitable name for Burke's outlook. In that expression, "liberalism" is the noun. It is primary. It communicates something about the house people are to make their homes in. The adjective "conservative" curbs the enthusiasm of liberalism but enhances its wisdom. Conservatism makes liberal

principles more practical, pertinent, and robust. It
grounds the arc of liberal civilization; it spans
continents; it can endure.[11]

While I am no conservative liberal in the mold of Burke, I
can see Burke's value. At a minimum, liberal doctrine is
commensurate with traditionalism insofar as liberalism seeks to
integrate other value systems peacefully.

Surely, therefore, Kingsnorth can do better than to get his
assessments of liberalism from close-minded theocrats like
Patrick Deneen.

The essence of liberalism is this: *Don't hack at my roots,
and I won't hack at yours. We might share some roots, you and I.
If so, let us work together in peace. If we do, an ordered ecosystem
might just spring up with plenty of soil left for others to grow in
their own way.*

One can only admire Kingsnorth's work because it's clear
he's grown. He writes beautifully and persuasively. I see why
there are certain features of life he wants to sacralize. That is
why I want him in the trenches next to us as we face both
Green's radical social-justice activists and Blue's Christ-
haunted theocrats. Those who learn to transcend and include
healthy first-tier values will ascend the spiral together. When we
do, we will figure out how to challenge the destructive
aspirations of Mean Green—or Greedy Orange, or
Fundamentalist Blue, or Bloodthirsty Red.

Hell, we might be able to help those under the spell of
radical social justice to leap from Green to Healthy Yellow. And
in the process, we can recall what is true, beautiful, and good in
Green.

CULTURAL EVOLUTION

"Ideas have sex," said fellow liberal Matt Ridley famously. The incredible bounty we enjoy each day is a consequence of this fact of human nature. Humans have ideas, and we transmit them to each other. Sometimes we adopt them and, perhaps more rarely, we hybridize our ideas to create something new. Each novel genome confers advantages or disadvantages within certain life conditions. This is perhaps no truer than in the domain of cultural evolution. One of the great liberal thinkers, Friedrich Hayek, offered us this insight.

If we squint hard enough at Hayek's theory of cultural evolution, we will see the *wisdom of rootedness* just as Kingsnorth did in the work of Simone Weil. In my own words, here's a summary of Hayek:

People transmit memes. Sometimes we adopt and imitate sociocultural memes. Among the most important memes are common rules and cultural norms that allow people to predict what others in their group will do. This provides order. Common rules and norms preserved over time become traditions. These are selected for and tested by our life conditions, which include competition with other groups. Traditions we might have imitated or adopted differ from instincts that evolved through biology. Sometimes this fact can make for conflicting internal thoughts or difficult external allegiances. Still, traditions can confer advantages to groups. Those traditions maintained through group selection can be superior to individual reason in certain respects because culture carries tacit adaptations to life conditions that a single mind could never apprehend. Though the precise mechanisms of biological and cultural evolution aren't exactly similar, they share relevant aspects. Both work through selection. Social rules persist through reproduction and fitness and get tested (and retested) by circumstances.

Traditionalists aren't likely to appreciate a Darwinian explanation of tradition's value—or, not at first blush—but at least the rationale shows how the Whig and the Tory might come to the same conclusion: *Don't mess with our roots.*

If this evolutionary view of cultural traditions is generally correct, what does this mean for radical social justice?

While radical social justice gained relatively rapid mindshare, it must quickly evolve. By analogy, certain viruses transmit quickly but also quickly destroy their hosts. Such viruses tend to die out, much in the same way that Marx's alpha variant did. Due to the destructive nature of radical social justice, people are developing a kind of immunity to Green's meaner memes. And hosts who find their lives worsened or destroyed won't long be effective propagation machines. Even as radical social-justice advocates are likely to gain political power in the short term, their values have little to no connection with the substrata.

FIGHT, FLIGHT, AND FACILITATE: A WAR ON THREE FRONTS

Finally, we arrive at our call to action. This call cannot be either/or. It must be yes-and.

First, traditionalists should join with liberals to fight radical social justice. But if by fight, we mean to use illiberal means, that risks creating a different, but equally dangerous, enemy.

Humbly, therefore, I submit that we lock arms in solidarity around original liberalism, which transcends and includes traditionalism.

Then, when we cannot fight, we must exit—that is, *flee*. It might sound cowardly, but it's not. Flight can mean leaving a state like California to settle in Texas or Arizona. Jurisdictional arbitrage is a way to let rotten cultures and institutions collapse while shoring up healthier institutions by voting with your feet.

Finally, we must help facilitate radical social-justice activists' cognitive and moral transition to a healthier place on the spiral. Some won't ever make it. But others will. And maybe, as Michael Strong referenced above, they will become leaders capable of seeing and synthesizing the healthier values of the whole spiral.

Integral thinking can lead us not only to a place of unity in pluralism favored by liberals but it can also work to the end of protecting our roots.

7
TOO COMPLEX FOR MISSION CONTROL

No economist I know thinks of the economy as being anything like a machine.
—Paul Krugman[1]

We need decentralization because only thus can we ensure that the knowledge of the particular circumstances of time and place will be promptly used.
—F. A. Hayek[2]

WELL INTO THE GREAT RECESSION, arch-Keynesian Paul Krugman wrote that what drew him to economics was "the beauty of pushing a button to solve problems."[3]

Yet economies don't have buttons.

Similarly, imagine someone who claimed she could build, fix, or run the Great Barrier Reef. You'd be justifiably skeptical. The Great Barrier Reef is one of the most splendid ecosystems on the planet. Its beauty is matched only by its complexity. No one on earth could design, much less control, the array of biological processes that allow the reef's fractal order to emerge.

If you believe in God's creation, you'd probably argue that only an omniscient being could build, fix, or run the Amazon Rain Forest. *Because humans aren't smart enough.* If you're an orthodox Darwinian, you'd argue that only the decentralized processes of evolution could give rise to such biodiversity. *Because humans aren't smart enough.*

Yet, for too long, we have tolerated experts who claim authority over our economies.

Sure, economy and ecology are two different domains of inquiry, but economies are like ecosystems in a few important respects. Both economies and ecosystems are complex adaptive systems that cannot be built, fixed, or run. Both emerge in their complexity thanks to simple rules. And both express unique patterns based on their particular contexts.

Despite these critical similarities, too many interventionists labor under the idea that economies are like machines that can be built, fixed, or run. Here is a handful of examples with my emphasis added:

- How Do We *Fix* the Economy? Modern Monetary Theory Explained[4]
- Five Ways to *Build* a Strong Economy[5]
- Labour are Much Better at *Running* the Economy than Voters Think[6]

Instead of enforcing stable institutional rules, interventionists think they have the knowledge required to meddle in the macroeconomy. Instead of respecting economic decisions distributed among those living in unique circumstances, interventionists deal in abstract aggregates and false metaphors.

I'm reminded of Bill Phillips, an older student at the London School of Economics (LSE) after World War II. Phillips built the Hydraulic Computer to model the UK's national economic processes. And despite the protestations of Paul Krugman, it not only suggests that Phillips's machine is like an economy, but that an economy is like a machine. The device might even give one the idea that economics is a discipline in which one can push a button to solve problems.

Larry Elliot, economics editor for *The Guardian*, describes the Phillips machine thus:

> The prototype was an odd assortment of tanks, pipes, sluices and valves, with water pumped around the machine by a motor cannibalised from the windscreen wiper of a Lancaster bomber. Bits of filed-down Perspex and fishing line were used to channel the coloured dyes that mimicked the flow of income round the economy into consumer spending, taxes, investment and exports. Phillips and Walter Newlyn, who helped piece the machine together at the end of the 1940s, experimented with treacle and methylated spirits before deciding that coloured water was the best way of displaying the way money circulates around the economy.[7]

Most write about the artifact in reverence, even as they admit the device was of its time. Today, they say, economists have computers to model the economy.

Nobel laureate Friedrich Hayek, known for his understanding of the economy as something decidedly more complex and organic, might quite literally have bumped into the thing. Hayek left LSE a year later, in 1950. One wonders what he thought of the device. I suspect he thought it was a conceit of technocracy and scientism, especially as the world would have to wait seven more years for Sputnik to kick off the space race.

MISSION CONTROL

Nearly everywhere, policymakers and central bankers manipulate our economies as if they were sitting at Mission Control. They fancy that if they can turn *this* dial or *that* rheostat, they'll be able to "prime the pump" or whatever inapt metaphor guides such hubris. Sadly, the only way technocrats have been able to take us to the moon since 1972 is atop a financial bubble.

In 2022, we began to hear a great hissing sound as malinvestment leaked from the "everything bubble." We have much further to fall. As of this writing, we continue to experience high inflation, despite the dollar and its exorbitant privilege. The inflation was not "transitory," as the authorities predicted. We share the experience of an ongoing global phenomenon that will compound our troubles quarter by quarter. Paradoxically, as the world plunges into recession, the dollar has gotten stronger for a time, due greatly to higher interest rates designed to destroy demand and lower asset prices. But that policy is something of an international wrecking ball, as weaker, more indebted nations compete for dollars to service their debts. This is but a snapshot.

In short: There is simply too much leverage in the global system. Something has to give.

Macroeconomic wizards, as well as the politicians into whose ears they whisper, have never faced the fact that economies are not like machines at all. Yet these economists' prestige, positions, and livelihoods depend on scientism. It's no wonder, then, that these self-same experts fail time and again to make basic predictions with any accuracy. Worse, they labor under the notion that, given enough power and largesse, they can play God by pushing buttons, bailing out banks, firing up the printing presses, or setting a different interest rate.

The bill always comes due—and eventually, it will be handed to you and your children.

MEDDLING BEGETS MEDDLING

President Richard Nixon took the U.S. dollar off the gold standard in 1971. Since then, macroeconomic entrail readers have been sowing the seeds of economic collapse by encouraging government profligacy as a cure for every ill. Specifically, Keynesians and their kissing cousins—the Modern Monetary Theorists—have been whispering sweet nothings into the ears of power. Tell the political class *exactly* what it wants to hear, and you might become a presidential appointee.

The fun usually starts with politicians eager to shower goodies on favor seekers. With Nixon, it was "guns and butter" funding for the welfare-warfare state. Today the only real difference is one of degree. Politicians are still fond of characterizing everything they do as an "investment" even though real investors have to feel the sting of losses. Neither politicians nor their consiglieres feel any sting or sign any IOUs. Indeed, most mandarins have no skin in the game.

Interest groups and constituents line up at the public trough. Dispensing corporate welfare and helicopter money becomes their raison d'etre. Intervention is a necessary evil for the common good, they'll say, brandishing their laurels from Harvard or the LSE. Only they, The Order of Macroeconomists, can rescue the economy from crisis to crisis.

Or so the story goes.

The wizards end up facilitating cronyism and corruption. One need only consider the billions the Fed has given to banks and other corporations during the past decade through quantitative easing, not to mention additional pains arising from the Cantillon Effect, a phenomenon in which all earlier-comers to newly created money—the privileged few, such as bankers—benefit directly, while later-comers like you and me suffer from inflation.

In response, populists yowl, and the people demand more goodies. But there is no more blood left in the turnip.

The mandarins of Mission Control have become adept at papering over these problems or, to mix metaphors, kicking the can beyond the next election cycle. Yet, meddling begets meddling. Eventually, the people must pay.

The wizards are not so good at setting impartial institutional protocols that allow the world's productive people to save, invest, produce, and exchange in a stable fiscal and monetary regime. To deny the wizards the power to adjust the price of credit (interest rate) would deny them an enormous lever. Most people can't imagine a world in which market actors determine such prices—you know, the same way we determine the price of eggs.

Instead, monetary interventionists sit behind an opaque marble facade and do their best to maintain *targets*, such as inflation and employment. The fiscal interventionists roam byzantine halls and smoky backrooms to determine which corporate cronies will win their masters' spending promises—you know, in the name of "creating jobs," or the "common good."

But neither politicians nor experts create wealth. They transfer it. And that sucking sound you hear comes from taxation and inflation.

THE DECENTRALIST IMPERATIVE

Whenever one complains about the sorry state of the world—including the all-too-visible hands behind the mess—a chorus of experts will reply:

But what shall be done? And who should do it?

These are not unreasonable questions, but they can mask certain assumptions. The most important of these is that a *particular* person ought to do *something*, which implies a centralized effort by some elite. That assumption scratches a distinctly human itch, which is to exert control or, at least, to feel that *someone* is in control. But the rage for order got us into this mess.

Authority's handmaidens will cry "market fundamentalism!" Yet what manner of faith says technocrats can or should play Intelligent Designer with our economies? What economic theory is more "trickle-down" than Keynesianism, obsessed as it is with stimulating aggregate demand? As Hayek taught us, dealing in aggregates completely misses the details—particularly the vital circumstances of time and place.

There are no angels among the mandarins. Legal counterfeiting is no manna. And neither the legislature nor the central bank is near the pearly gates.

That's why anyone who purports to know the *right* way, much less the *One True Way*, should have to enter a vast competition for mindshare, attracting members to their systems rather than compelling them. So my position isn't market fundamentalism at all. It's about market fundamentals.

The best systems win by creating long-term value for those they claim to serve. If Switzerland beats Somalia, more people will choose the former. Competition among systems makes for a more "antifragile" metasystem, following grumpy Taleb. Failures are localized. Watchful stewards can duplicate successes.

We must therefore enter an Age of Consent in which we choose our monetary systems from a menu of providers who must respond to customers rather than to the powerful. And if they don't? People will simply vote with their boats.

THE MONETARY-INSTITUTIONAL STACK

Imagine what we might call the monetary-institutional stack. In that stack, you have the issuers, such as independent banks, cryptocurrency networks, or smaller states. Some will adopt commodity standards, such as gold or a basket/index of commodities. Others will adopt a bitcoin standard. Still others will generate algorithmic stablecoins or currencies that continuously improve based on feedback from the fitness landscape.

Click out an order of magnitude from these issuers, and you'll find authorities operating in various jurisdictions— perhaps 50—after America breaks up, or in the UK after Scottish or Welsh secession. Some of these new authorities will successfully regulate issuers operating within those jurisdictions. Others will not be so successful or will choose market discipline. But at that level of the monetary-institutional stack, there is competition. After a time, we'll see arbitrageurs do what they do on the way to more stable equilibria—for example, as we did in Canada's or Scotland's eras of free banking.

Monetary economists Selgin and White study the empirics of America's central bank's history and conclude:

The Fed's full history (1914 to present) has been characterized by more rather than fewer symptoms of monetary and macroeconomic instability than the decades leading to the Fed's establishment.[8]

Selgin and White are rare because they deviate from the Mission Control approach and so they recommend decentralized competition among currency issuers. They understand that better ways must be discovered, not compelled, in a Darwinian dance.

If we fail to underthrow the central banking regime and transition before collapse, brutal circumstances will make a transition for us as the empire's macroeconomic machine sputters and stalls.

Evolutionary processes, though potentially painful in the short term, will select for superior money and governance—as judged by participants. Decentralization will catalyze this process as issuers compete. The competition will center on desired properties, as opposed to the interests of the powerful.

In terms of the desire for political types to transfer opportunities to favored groups, the decentralization of money and authority makes that game much less profitable. Accountability gets baked in when switching costs go down. Suppose the costs of voting with your Honda or your smartphone continue to go down as our great experiments in centralization unravel. In that case, we'll see competitive forces exert themselves to benefit the people over the powerful.

We seek a system that operates according to "the consent of the governed." By now, you probably recognize that this doesn't mean majoritarian rule. It means a real, contractual civil association that a sovereign person selects in a governance market. But let there be no illusions. Power will do what power does, and the powerful will try to disrupt the process. Still, as the inevitable forces of decentralization check power, authorities will have to content themselves with controlling less but providing more. That means fewer imperial ambitions, smaller territories, and more sustainable budgets.

THE BIG ONE

The next recession might well be a depression. The Federal Reserve has run out of tricks and sits on the tines of the devil's fork: raise interest rates too high, and we'll see mass layoffs, unaffordable mortgage rates, and weaker governments unable to service their debts; keep printing money, and we'll see our purchasing power continue to diminish. We can say something similar about the European Central Bank and Bank of England. The U.S. government is currently sloshing about in an ocean of red ink at nearly 140 percent of GDP, though the dollar is still the world's reserve currency.

The days of exorbitant privilege seem nigh at an end.

The Bretton Woods era is nearly done. The Fed's power is waning. Europe is a basket case. The Great Reset is a technocratic nightmare devised by those still clinging to unholy corporatist hierarchies and green hysteria. Xi's attempts to sinoform the world aren't exactly going as planned, either. All such efforts will be weakened by the coming upheaval—which means it will be time to reorganize according to different economic principles among smaller, competing systems.

Instead of what amounts to the economics profession's

version of Intelligent Design, we need a set of practical experiments constrained by economic reality, stable rules, and distributed decision-making. We'll need more Singapores and Liechtensteins, some on terra firma, others in the Cloud.

Let the empires fall.

8

A LITTLE REBELLION NOW
AND THEN IS A GOOD THING

---

*Governments derive their just powers from the consent of
the governed. You have neither solicited nor received ours.*
—John Perry Barlow[1]

WHEN IT COMES TO POLITICS, the left-right dimension has
become nearly unrecognizable. At one extreme, a mob shouts,
loots, topples, and cancels. At the other extreme, reactionaries,
theocrats, and trolls cheer strongmen. The rest—the bell of the
curve—picks a team and watches from the bleachers.

That is, except for the liberals:

- We liberals have always prized *voice*, but the air has
  become toxic with bad discourse.
- We liberals have always sought *exit*, but now there's
  really nowhere to go.
- We liberals have always been *loyal*, but to ideals
  rather than a patch of soil.

And we are in retreat.

It feels like we're on the front cusp of a dark age. The relevant political axis is liberal-authoritarian, but too few care about this distinction, if they even know what it means. Politics has degenerated. Rival gangs war over mindshare, poised to seize control of a great protection racket. That means true liberals can no longer afford to be half-hearted. Instead, we have to figure out how to harness the power of exit, voice, and loyalty, or things will get a hell of a lot more dystopian.

In the fifty years since the publication of Albert Hirschman's masterwork, *Exit, Voice, and Loyalty*, innovators have created new recipes that realize his tripartite human algorithm: Social media offered amateurs a new kind of megaphone; cryptocurrencies offered a monetary escape hatch; network effects create grudging-but-powerful loyalties. For all the marginal technological improvements, we still haven't quite been able to self-organize in parallel with Leviathan.

But we have to.

THE JEFFERSONIAN FIRE

Adam Thierer, in an essay for the fiftieth anniversary of Hirschman's book, writes:

If technological innovation can help us check governments' worst tendencies and improve the quality of our public policies and institutions—all without resorting to radical action—then there is a strong moral case for defending it.[2]

Maybe Thierer and I have very different conceptions of

"radical action," but I think there is a far stronger moral case for radicalism than mere checks and balances. If the unprecedented levels of spending and debt weren't enough to justify it, maybe the disquieting expansion of the police, surveillance, and censorship states is a reminder that "a little rebellion now and then is a good thing."

We need more of that Jeffersonian fire.

I don't mean that we ought to take weapons to Washington. Nor should we run into the streets to chant slogans. Instead, we need to be *constructive* revolutionaries, accelerating those innovations most likely to undermine the apparatuses of state power. We can do this by developing protocols of subversion that will have a cumulative decentralizing effect. Because with every successive generation, federal power grows. And its growth seems to be inversely proportional to Americans' belief in liberalism.

Thierer thinks innovation should be about keeping policy "fresh" and "sensible." The apotheosis of Thierer's "permissionless innovation," then, is to "help make public officials more responsive to the people by reining in the excesses of the administrative state, making government more transparent and accountable, and ensuring that our civil rights and economic liberties are respected."

Heavens no.

The point is not to make public officials more responsive. It's to make them redundant. The goal is not to rein in the excesses of the administrative state. It's to obviate it. Nor is it just to make the government more transparent and accountable, but rather to establish protocols of self-organization that make Leviathan entirely obsolete.

As complexity scientist Yaneer Bar-Yam writes,

> Why should governments fail? Because leaders, whether self-appointed dictators, or elected officials, are unable to identify what policies will be good for a complex society. The unintended consequences are beyond their comprehension. Regardless of values or objectives, the outcomes are far from what they intend.[3]

There is a solution. It is not a form of government, no "ism" or "ocracy" will do. It begins with widespread individual action that transforms society—a metamorphosis of social organization in which leadership no longer serves the role it has over millennia. A different type of existence will emerge, affecting all of us as individuals and enabling us to live in a complex world.

Bar-Yam sees a complexity transition[4] in which we leave political and organizational hierarchies behind in favor of systems of decentralized teamwork. As society becomes more complex, there are two choices before us: decentralization or collapse.

Even if we fall short of such ambitions in our lifetimes, we have to try. Threatening violence against innocents to realize your notion of the good doesn't work very well. It's also wrong. And yet authoritarianism is back in fashion. So, at least I agree partly with erstwhile liberal Peter Thiel, who wrote, "we are in a deadly race between politics and technology."

For now, I'll pass over the disturbing possibility that politicians will accelerate technological means of expanding their control.

GREEN LIGHTS

Maybe I misunderstood permissionless innovation, I thought. It turns out I had. Here's how Adam Thierer explains it:

For innovation to blossom, entrepreneurs need a clear green light from policymakers that signals a general acceptance of risk-taking, especially risk-taking that challenges existing business models and traditional ways of doing things.

We can think of this disposition as "permissionless innovation" and if there was one thing every policymaker could do to help advance long-term growth, it would be to commit themselves to advancing this ethic and making it the lodestar for all their future policy pronouncements and decisions.[5]

Before reading the above passage, I thought permissionless innovation surely meant the kinds of innovations that geeks and dreamers could create and the rest of us could adopt *without getting anyone's permission.* Can you imagine if Jefferson or John Perry Barlow had written "The Entreaty of Independence"? If we are to sit around and wait for some authority, whose power depends on the status quo, to give us a "clear green light" to upend the status quo, there will never be meaningful, lasting social change.

A pressing question for Thierer is *if there is no green light, what happens?* So let's get beyond Thierer's "permissionless innovation." What I have in mind is a bit more radical.

SUBVERSIVE INNOVATION

Maybe I'm just getting impatient in my old age. Still, whether one desires fresh, sensible policy or bold experiments in human self-organization, we're getting too little of either. Instead, we're getting an unhealthy excess of voice, too few opportunities to exit, and a lot of misguided loyalty to two parties who care only about having power. Our neglected liberal order has become dry kindling between two extremist groups—one with tiki torches and the other with Molotov cocktails. Staring down $32 trillion in debt and much more in unfunded liabilities, we could be less than a decade from either collapse or civil war.

We need a different kind of revolution.

We can no longer labor under the sentimental notions of "voice," such as voter enfranchisement and public service. We should all know our public choice by now. Even if most voters had a sense of history, restraint, or civic consciousness, representative government would still be a mirage. To the extent that elections reflect voter preferences, these amount to an incoherent blur. Too many voters now have a greater appetite for tribal domination. Such leads me to wonder why any liberal would want to "make public officials more responsive," as if all we are talking about is fixing potholes or shortening the line at the DMV.

When it comes to subversive innovation, we seem to be stuck on the same old examples: Uber. Airbnb. Bitcoin. That was a good start, but we need a tidal wave of novelty. New tools. New rules. Simple, accessible, and ready for mass adoption. These innovations will create new institutional forms and communities of practice into which millions of adopters can flow—especially if things keep going downhill. If a critical mass of constituencies adopts these innovations, we have a hope of inverting the process of concentrated benefits and dispersed costs. We can't forget voice or loyalty, of course. But we need to invest a lot more in exit.

UNDERTHROW

The best way to honor *Exit, Voice and Loyalty*, then, is to think of it as a manual. Like the rest of our liberalism, we must take what is now perceived as a rather bloodless set of maxims and rules and transform these into *active practices*. We can't afford to wait around for authoritarian mind viruses to recede with the electoral tides. Again, we must engage not in overthrow but in underthrow, which requires more than tut-tutting on social media. Otherwise, the thumbs under which we already live will become unbearably heavy, as they have for the people of Hong Kong and mainland China.

I wrote in my book The Social Singularity: Every innovation is an act of subversion.

Just before Satoshi Nakamoto published his 2008 white paper on the rudiments of Bitcoin, it must have been a bit like holding a lit match over dry forest underbrush. Did he linger for a moment before hitting enter?

Maybe in that moment he closed his eyes and saw flashes from the future: of a thousand pimply geeks becoming millionaires overnight. Of Ross Ulbricht, Silk Road's Dread Pirate Roberts, being led away in handcuffs. Of mutant strains, copycats, forks, and tokens competing in an entire ecosystem of cryptocurrencies as in a digital coral reef. Of booms and busts and troughs of disillusionment.

We don't know. But we do know one thing about
Satoshi Nakamoto: he hit enter.[6]

Satoshi Nakamoto was a radical. The bitcoin white paper is
exit, voice, and loyalty in one: the blueprints to escape our
imposed systems of central banking (exit); nine pages of pure
cypherpunk expression that inspired an army of coders (voice),
and an implicit commitment to liberalism, that cosmopolitan
ideal enshrined in the Bill of Rights (loyalty).

We need more Satoshis.

PRACTICE LIBERALISM

So, how can we turn exit, voice, and loyalty into active
practices?

Exit: It's not enough to leave for Panama, Switzerland, or
Malta. It's not enough to pay lip service to Amendments Nine
and Ten. We must set about creating technologies that facilitate
new markets in governance:

- Let's create special economic zones like Prospera,
  startup societies, even parallel jurisdictions of
  "cloud governance."
- Let's build new systems of schooling, healthcare,
  and mutual aid, many of which will be decoupled
  from any territory.
- Let's create new power-shifted corporate
  management systems and governance like
  holacracy, including dynamic equity shares and
  cooperative ownership structures.

In other words, we must innovate in both polycentric law

and panarchy. Because even if we cannot adopt these systems wholesale today, we want them to exist when the checks don't cash, a cup of coffee costs $100, and America's Cultural Revolution has run its course.

Voice: Voting in national elections is like yelling at two bad teams from the nosebleed section at Madison Square Garden. That is not a system worth preserving, even with blockchain voting. We are living in the era of memetic warfare, and liberalism is losing. So:

- We have to get more creative, artful, and ennobling with our messages—not only so we can capture more mindshare, but also so we can offer a spiritual home to those who are more interested in human progress than meme wars.
- We have to bring about a great media hard fork— such as the decentralized web and social media—so that dissident voices can't be deplatformed by government functionaries or private censors. We will have to tolerate conspiracies and offensive speech, but we can train ourselves to be more discerning and filter out the nonsense.
- We have to insist on liberal rules of inquiry, including standards of rationality and evidence that work against authoritarian assertions— whether from critical theorists or political hacks. Otherwise, voice will continue to serve power.

There may come a day, though, when the time for talk is over.

Loyalty: July 4th is to most Americans what Christmas is to most Americans: an excuse to eat a lot and forget why you're celebrating. We must recommit to the ideas that animated the

American founding—and build on them. This isn't empty patriotism. It requires thoughtful reflection and the cultivation of liberal virtue. Our mantra is and must always be *Libertas perfundet omnia luce* (Freedom will flood all things with light). And we have to turn this form of loyalty into new expressions of civil disobedience, nonviolent resistance, and organizational transformation. If we don't hasten a liberal renaissance, we will find ourselves reduced to an inscription on Ozymandias's pedestal.

A liberal renaissance will also require us to improve upon liberalism itself. One big reason liberalism is in decline is that it has become a rather lifeless collection of rules, some of which were written down in what used to be a functional social operating system.[7] To the American Founders, these ideas had been a secular religion. Over time, though, fewer and fewer Americans venerate them. So maybe it's time we looked east.

FEAR IS THE ENEMY

Maybe you've heard the term *ahimsa* from the Vedic traditions. Ahimsa is the practice of nonviolence in thought, word, and deed. It requires discipline and patience. Libertarian adherents to Mill's Harm Principle or the homelier Non-Aggression Principle will do well to look to the Buddhists and Jains who *practice* ahimsa because practice goes deeper than principle. Practice, after all, is a conscious and continuous commitment to right action, which can be infectious to those around you.

Though it seems contradictory, we need civility and civil disobedience at the same time. It is through such practice that we make good trouble. Ahimsa first, then *satyagraha* (truth force), animated Gandhi in his courageous struggles against the British Empire in India. It animated James Morris Lawson, Jr.

and Martin Luther King, Jr. during the Civil Rights era. And it can animate every coder, legal scholar, and organizational innovator who dares to compete with the state by offering new governance products. So, by Jeffersonian fire, we don't mean "refreshing the tree of liberty with the blood of patriots and tyrants." We mean, "Power based on love is a thousand times more effective and permanent than the one derived from fear of punishment."

A lot of liberals think that government is the enemy.

It's no wonder, as writer Jamie Bartlett puts it, "Nation-states rely on control." And fear is control's lever. But Bartlett adds:

If they can't control information, crime, businesses, borders or the money supply, then they will cease to deliver what citizens demand of them. In the end, nation-states are nothing but agreed-upon myths: we give up certain freedoms in order to secure others. But if that transaction no longer works, and we stop agreeing on the myth, it ceases to have power over us.[8]

Maybe our true enemy, then, is fear. It's fear that causes us humbly to request a green light. It's fear that keeps us from trying new things. And it's fear that makes us submit to the urge to control. The more we lock arms in solidarity, the less afraid we'll be. It's time for liberals to go from being passive adherents of an abstract doctrine to being active practitioners recreating society.

Our three paths are exit, voice, or loyalty.

9
CAN WE HAVE WELFARE WITHOUT THE THREAT OF VIOLENCE?

Mutual aid ... is the surest means for giving to each and to all the greatest safety, the best guarantee of existence and progress, bodily, intellectual and moral.
—Pyotr Kropotkin[1]

MOST GROWNUPS DON'T BELIEVE in magic anymore. Sometimes, though, it can be helpful to imagine it. A powerful ring turns the wearer invisible in J. R. R. Tolkien's *The Lord of the Rings*. That power means the wearer can act with relative impunity. (For that device, Tolkien had Plato to thank.)

We can also imagine characters with superhuman abilities. These thought experiments sometimes help us put ourselves and our societies into perspective. In Tolkien's world, we wrestle with questions about the nature of power. In our world, we can explore the nature of peace.

Let's imagine that wizards exist in our world, and one supremely powerful wizard has cast a spell over the realm.

THE SPELL OF NONVIOLENCE

The wizard's spell is of nonviolence. Call it "The Spell of Ahimsa." Under this spell, no one can threaten or commit any act that injures another person or their property. When a brigand tries to attack a caravan on the road, his fingers weaken, and his dagger simply falls from his grasp. When a tax collector tries to arrest a merchant in the town, the handcuffs slip from his fingers. When a bully tries to push another girl, she discovers an invisible wall of protection. It doesn't matter whether the perpetrator *thinks* he is using violence to serve good or evil. The fact is, the spell ensures a condition of complete nonviolence in society.

What should we make of this? Would the realm be better off under the wizard's spell?

Answers will vary. Nearly every society has laws against theft, fraud, and physical injury, which means something is justifiable about the spell. So at least a fair number of people might agree intuitively that the world would be better without violence. As soon as we get into questions about the justification for authority's threats of violence, though, answers start to diverge.

Differences are starkest when we think of the spell affecting government officials. Consider The Spell of Ahimsa as it relates to issues of government-issued welfare. In other words, if the wizard used magic such that officials had to abstain from violence, how would authorities implement redistribution schemes? Specifically, how would authorities tax the rich to give to the poor?

REDISTRIBUTION AS ROOTED IN VIOLENCE

The redistributive state is a recent phenomenon in history. In fact, what made the welfare state affordable was the rapid advances of industry and enterprise. After about 1800, this advance—known as the "hockey stick"[2] of prosperity—helped generate opportunities for people to create more value for one another. For maybe the first time in history, there were more people trading than raiding. People living in this Great Enrichment rocketed out of poverty.

According to economic historian Deirdre McCloskey:

> Earlier prosperities had intermittently increased real income per head by double or even triple, 100 or 200 percent or so, only for it to fall back to the miserable $3 a day typical of humans since the caves. But the Great Enrichment increased real income per head, in the face of a rise in the number of heads, by a factor of seven— by anything from 2,500 to 5,000 percent.[3]

A few entrepreneurs got amazingly wealthy in the Great Enrichment, but a massive middle class emerged, too, as people figured out how to organize themselves into productive firms. These firms weren't perfect, but they were responsible for unprecedented improvements in living standards. With such gains, even the poorest improved their lot.

In the late nineteenth and early twentieth centuries, governments began instituting welfare programs and other centralized forms of social welfare. Beyond Bismarck's cynical gambit to buy votes and beat the Socialists, the exoteric notion had been to see to the basic needs of the least fortunate. But these systems brought along a set of perverse consequences. And as these systems began to predominate, existing voluntary systems of civil society disappeared. Essential features of voluntary systems, such as the *practice* of compassion and community, not to mention the development of personal responsibility, slowly disappeared along with them.

The Spell of Ahimsa helps us see a feature of the redistributive welfare state that is frequently overlooked: *its very existence depends on state-sanctioned violence.* In other words, how would the system operate if authorities couldn't threaten to imprison those who refused to pay for it?

Most people don't think about matters this way, accustomed to the idea of the welfare state as a permanent fixture of life. But as we will see, it hasn't always been this way. Human beings naturally organize themselves.

SAVINGS CLUBS AROUND THE WORLD

Tanomoshi is a locally organized system of mutual aid. These community resource pools have existed in Japan at least since the middle Kamakura period of 1185 to 1333 BCE.[4] Under this system, each member would contribute a small sum at regular intervals and would receive a single, lump payment whenever the member experienced a significant life event.

In medieval Japan, per-capita GDP is estimated to have been between 500 and 800 dollars in 2011 dollars.[5] (Compare this with today's U.S. poverty level of $12,880 for a single person.) Every month, people would travel to the *tanomoshiko* to leave a little bit of money. A trusted party there would accept their contribution with a bow. *Tanomoshiko* is translated as "reliable group," so the community selected a steward of integrity. Though most medieval Japanese earned very little, they were committed. One family might have arranged for a daughter to be married. Another might have found a parent has become gravely ill. Each would be able to go directly to the *tanomoshiko* for support.

In some of the poorest parts of the world, there is little capacity for government welfare, let alone modern banking. So in places like sub-Saharan Africa, people contribute a modest monthly allotment to a *su su* (or sou-sou). Those who aren't very good at saving money by themselves are encouraged to use a *su su* because club members hold one another accountable.

Here's how it works, according to South African writer Lihle Z. Mtshali, describing the Afro-Caribbean variant in America:

The group elects a treasurer who will collect the members' contributions. She will also create a payout roster, or members can request to receive their hand at any given date during the cycle. Everyone agrees on how much and how often they want to contribute. If ten members are contributing $100 a week, each week a member will receive a $1,000 hand or cash lump sum. The cycle begins again after ten weeks. Any member who can afford it can also double their contribution and get paid two hands in one cycle.[6]

Because there is no interest to be collected, members always get out the exact amount they put in. The recipient changes each period in a rotating fashion such that every member of the group is eventually a recipient.

Curiously, this arrangement has sprung up in various forms worldwide throughout history.

A similar system called *kye* in Korea is still around today, even among Korean immigrants to the U.S. Similar rotational systems include *tandas* (Latin America), *cundinas* (Mexico), *partnerhand* (Caribbean/UK), *hui* (Asia), *Game'ya* (Middle East), *pandeiros* (Brazil), and *arisan* (Indonesia). These systems facilitate personal savings, investment in property and enterprise, insurance, personal loans, and assistance to poorer people. In developed countries, people can use these systems to build credit.

MUTUAL AID IN AMERICA

Today, if you were to ask the average man or woman on the street to name a mutual aid society, you would be lucky if he or she could name a single one. But at one time in America these organizations were everywhere. They had funny names like the Oddfellows, the Free African Society, and the Brotherhood of Locomotive Engineers. At one time, they included health insurance and unemployment support. Because they were a mix of the communitarian and the charitable, surplus dues could go to growth and giving. As most organized into local chapters and lodges, they featured the undocumented acts of kindness and tough love we would scarcely recognize if we saw today. They are the forgotten social safety net.

This vast empire of human good was built not by federal largesse but on the moral conviction of free people weaving their lives together as a community to guard against hardship. Once held together by tight neighborhoods, mutual support, and barn raisings, a communitarian society has been torn apart by redistribution. Beholden to banks or bureaucracies, most Americans are dependent on the plans of authorities thousands of miles away. The rest are compelled to foot the bill—*or else*. At one stage, this system was affordable. But in time, the system became corrosive and dependent on public and private debt.

As we have fallen deeper into debt, we have forgotten how to take care of one another. The rise of the administrative welfare state corresponds to civil society's decline. Whether it's correlation or causation, I cannot say. But the circumstantial evidence is pretty damning.

THE DECLINE OF COMMUNITY

When Alexis de Tocqueville came to America in 1831, he saw something profound. Maybe you've read the following passage before. But as you read it again, ask yourself whether or to what degree this is an America you recognize:

> The political associations that exist in the United States are only a single feature in the midst of the immense assemblage of associations in that country. Americans of all ages, all conditions, and all dispositions constantly form associations. They have not only commercial and manufacturing companies, in which all take part, but associations of a thousand other kinds, religious, moral, serious, futile, general or restricted, enormous or diminutive. The Americans make associations to give entertainments, to found seminaries, to build inns, to construct churches, to diffuse books, to send missionaries to the antipodes; in this manner they found hospitals, prisons, and schools. If it is proposed to inculcate some truth or to foster some feeling by the encouragement of a great example, they form a society. Wherever at the head of some new undertaking you see the government in France, or a

man of rank in England, in the United States you will
be sure to find an association.[7]

There is not much left of Tocqueville's America.

Reading Tocqueville, one can imagine a time when the
organs of civil association extended to spheres of life such as
childhood and old age. But these are institutionalized and
segregated today. Children are warehoused by the state so that
parents can work to pay bills and taxes. The elderly are similarly
warehoused and told more or less that their participation in
productive society is optional after age 65. Beyond that point,
many become liabilities to be managed by the Congressional
Budget Office.

Consider, then, the lost array of mutual aid societies,
lodges, and fraternal orders of which a third of Americans were
once members. Historian David Beito painstakingly
investigates a handful of these to offer a clearer picture:

The record of five societies that thrived at or near the
turn of the century illustrates the many variants of this
system. Each had a distinct membership base. Two of
the societies, the Independent Order of Saint Luke
and the United Order of True Reformers, were all-
black. Both had been founded by ex-slaves after the
Civil War and specialized initially in sickness and
burial insurance. The other societies had entirely
white memberships. The Loyal Order of Moose was
an exclusively male society that emphasized sickness
and burial benefits. It became best known during the
20th century for its orphanage, Mooseheart, near
Aurora, Illinois. The Security Benefit Association

(originally the Knights and Ladies of Security) followed in a similar tradition but broke from the mainstream by allowing men and women to join on equal terms.[8]

Even as we shake our modern heads at segregation along racial lines, we can still appreciate the power of civil association that has all but disappeared in the twenty-first century.

There is no doubt that most human beings care for others. This care can extend to strangers. At some level, we all want to be *assured* that poor people can get help when they need it. Most of us want to know that those who seek our help *really need it* and that assistance doesn't create dependency. Mutual aid societies served this function because members kept an eye on other members.

Government welfare views successful people as human ATMs and the poor as statistical plot points. There is no discernment. A mutual-aid renaissance would discourage people from simply outsourcing their compassion. Instead, we would all have to learn to be compassionate again.

THE FUNDAMENTAL QUESTIONS

In an age of rapid technological advances and material abundance, we must ask penetrating questions about whether the current sociopolitical order is morally justifiable.

First, if you *could* choose nonviolent means of achieving social goals such as poverty relief, wouldn't you? After all, violence causes suffering. Causing unnecessary suffering against innocent people is wrong.

One might respond by arguing that nonviolent forms of poverty relief are impossible, so the extent to which the relatively well-off suffer from taxation is a necessary evil. But isn't this line of argument just a failure of imagination? If such a striking level of conscientiousness and compassion could take root in medieval Japan, one wonders what might spring up in this age of prosperity. Remember that mutual aid was robust in the past without the benefits of modern technology and material abundance. It's easier to dispel skepticism about voluntary arrangements when we reflect on mutual aid in the era of digital ledgers. (Remember, we haven't yet discussed the improvements to the charity sector that the Internet has enabled.)

Now, if we can demonstrate that mutual aid and charity could be robust enough to help the least advantaged, wouldn't that mean the violent redistributive state causes unnecessary suffering?

Advocates for the welfare state sometimes argue that wealthier members of society don't suffer all that much when authorities compel them through taxation. But if we agree that the goal is to help the poor rather than to hurt the rich, then we should stay focused on poverty alleviation. We've allowed ourselves to become distracted by envy and indignation, which actually hinders our efforts. Moreover, the vast majority of the wealthy's assets don't go to consumption but rather to capital, which itself fuels other poverty-fighting endeavors such as investments in companies and a thousand experiments in effective altruism.

Capital is never idle—notwithstanding the perverse distortions created by central banks.

Finally, if it's possible to help the poor (and for the poor to help each other) without resorting to violence, isn't this something we ought to do? If so, we have a moral obligation to transition away from the violent welfare state to a nonviolent condition of community support, charity, and mutual aid.

Sadly, moral suasion isn't likely to work. But if governments around the world find they can no longer afford the bloat and unprecedented debt, it could be that mutual aid is the last remaining option.

According to *Reuters*, global debt now stands at more than 300 percent of the world's GDP.[9]

BECOMING THE SOCIAL SAFETY NET

We have demonstrated that mutual aid is possible and potentially more effective than government welfare, even among the poorest people. Even if a subset cannot participate in mutual aid, the least advantaged would still be able to rely more on families, churches, charities, and communities—all of which would likely provide greater support compared to the status quo.

Advocates of state welfare might object that communities, charities, and mutual aid offer no guarantees. Yet after a century of welfare-state transfers, there are still no guarantees. The so-called safety net has become a sticky web of dependency on resources the powerful provide through violent means. And this has become unsustainable. The tragedy of this sorry chapter is that the state monopoly on welfare has strangled innumerable welfare-enhancing projects in their cradles. This invisible graveyard of potential has almost no constituency to fight for it, much less create it in the future.

Mutual-aid arrangements are not superior just because they are voluntary. These systems build in mechanisms of accountability and integrity for members—the practice of compassion. By contrast, government welfare is impersonal and treats everyone the same, reducing incentives to work and engendering an unhealthy sense of entitlement.

Still, the least advantaged are far more likely to find good options without a vast government welfare empire. In 1900, when U.S. per-capita GDP was only $4,000, one third of American men belonged to a mutual-aid society. Just think what this sector could look like with an average per-capita GDP of $65,000—with only about 11 percent living below the federal poverty level.

Again, the debt spending that is needed to prop up the welfare system continuously has created risks of a global meltdown.

The mutual-aid sector is thus due for a renaissance. It might seem radical, but charity and mutual-aid systems create more trust, engender more integrity, and offer greater responsibility. Suppose, though, that the compulsory redistribution system continues to grow. In that case, there will be fewer opportunities for experimentation in mutual aid— that is, until the economy drowns in a sea of red ink.

CASTING THE SPELL

Sadly, as it turns out, there is no Spell of Ahimsa. It is impossible to cast such a spell on everyone. But one thing is possible: You and I can cast this spell on ourselves.

We can form a moral community of people who refuse to support institutions that threaten violence to operate. I'd be willing to bet that where there is more peace, there is also more compassion.

As more people cast this spell upon themselves, we will find we live in a world of increased dignity, flourishing, and love.

10

TRUST IS BUSTED. BUST THE TRUST

To the men in Washington, the world is just a giant Monopoly board.
—Woody Harrelson[1]

As A BOY, one of the recurring themes in my social studies books was that monopolies are bad. I learned that a few big ones had sprung up during America's Gilded Age and that "robber barons" were to blame—that is until trust busters astride white horses came to the rescue.

History's a funny thing. Remember all those eighth-grade tall tales about how FDR's New Deal got us out of the Great Depression? Tales of Gilded Age trusts and trust-busting are sometimes just as tall. Generally speaking, though, almost everyone across the political spectrum agrees that monopolies are less than ideal.

Monopolies, especially government-sanctioned ones, create barriers to entry that make it nearly impossible for new entrants to compete. Because there is little to no competition, a monopoly can set prices far above what it could expect in more competitive conditions. A monopoly can also degrade the quality or change the quantity of a good or service. There are almost no substitutes for monopoly-provided products, so consumers have no alternatives. So, a single seller will offer poor-quality products or bad customer service at high prices.

While reasonable people will disagree about how monopolies form and what should be done about them, almost everyone agrees that market competition is better for everyone. After all, competition creates incentives for organizations to offer higher quality at a lower price.

TRUST IS BUSTED

When I think about monopolies, I'm reminded of this now-classic passage from philosopher Michael Huemer:

> Imagine that someone proposed that the key to establishing social justice and restraining corporate greed was to establish a very large corporation, much larger than any corporation hitherto known—one with revenues in the trillions of dollars. A corporation that held a monopoly on some extremely important market within our society. And used its monopoly in that market to extend its control into other markets. And hired men. with guns to force customers to buy its product at whatever price it chose. And periodically bombed the employees and customers of corporations in other countries.

What an awful vision. You might see how people would quickly lose trust in this corporation.

Huemer continues:

"By what theory would we predict that this corporation, above all others, could be trusted to serve our interests and to protect us both from criminals and from all the other corporations? If someone proposed to establish a corporation like this, would your trepidation be assuaged the moment you learned that every adult would be issued one share of stock in this corporation, entitling them to vote for members of the board of directors?"[2]

Readers who have had their coffees will notice Huemer is referring to the government. The question becomes—if our current system isn't really so different from Huemer's description—why does anyone trust a national government to protect and serve the rest of society?

BUST THE TRUST

You'd think people would see the benefits of real competition in governance. Even though there is not nearly enough variation among our fifty options, states with more favorable tax and business climates tend to attract more enterprising people. Nice weather never hurts, but it's not the only factor. Despite only slight variation among their respective institutions, think about how much competition there is for Americans among the fifty U.S. states. New Yorkers have been moving to North Carolina in droves. Californians have been snatching up homes and starting new businesses in Texas. New Hampshire and Florida vie for the title of America's freest state, which benefits both states as migrants seek greener pastures.

Still, more localism in governance options means we can do better than outsource our concerns to authorities far, far away. It's not merely that we could. We should. People would enjoy more rights to organize into their chosen communities or systems instead of engaging in factionalism and partisan strife. Such strife threatens social unrest, especially as each faction wants to dominate. As the Hollywood harridan, Kathy Griffin, wrote in the lead-up to the 2022 midterm election, "If you don't want a Civil War, vote for Democrats in November. If you do want a Civil War, vote Republican."[3]

Such woeful binary thinking reinforces unnecessary partisan warfare. Our hypothesis is that if people have more options, they'll have less to fight over. The Kathy Griffins of the world could stay in their zip codes and show up to the Town Hall.

It wouldn't matter if you formed a small kibbutz, a fraternal society, or a free private city. What matters is an institutionalized right of self-determination. Governance pluralism would follow. In the interests of a grand compromise, even modest decentralization creates more opportunities for people to eat their ideological cake and have it, too. The only cost of such a compromise comes in no longer being able to impose the One True Way onto everyone else—in a great multilateral agreement.

But that would mean getting rid of the Federal Government as we know it. For international readers, it probably means a more serious challenge to the powers-that-be in your corner of the world, too.

To a lot of partisans, this idea will seem downright crazy,

which goes to show just how upside-down the world has become. The Founder's federalism is called extremist. Centralized power is en vogue. Strange how the rabid activists for central authority froth when they call those with whom they disagree, fascists! But to save some vestige of our liberal experiment, we need *more* experiments, not fewer.

Experimentation in governance is the essence of polycentrism.

Thomas Jefferson's timeless warnings are as relevant today as they were in 1789. Whether or not you consider the Declaration a legal companion to America's founding charter, I hope to persuade you, at least, that at its core lies a cosmopolitan ideal. Philosophers can quibble about theological justifications for basic rights. As long as we secure them, we can justify them in any number of ways. The underappreciated point here, which we must reinforce, is *consent*. Prior to that, we have to figure out the mode and manner of America's partition into smaller jurisdictions.

Breaking up is hard to do, but it's not that hard.

More institutional pluralism means more opportunities for local participation. What might that look like? Peaceful secession? A loose confederation? More federalism? We will still be Americans even if we let people experiment and be united in the project of experimentation. Let the democratic socialists turn Vermont into an egalitarian, buy-local paradise. Let Northern California break off from the San Francisco Bay area to form the Free State of Jefferson. Let New Hampshire become even freer. Even if Austin "keeps it weird" as an independent city-state, let the Republic of Texas separate.

This is nothing new. And it works.

Polycentric legal frameworks like those already working in Switzerland should at least help us localize tug-of-war-style politics. We don't have to stop trading with one another—and we shouldn't. But we do have to stop imposing monolithic systems upon people who prefer to live in a different political, cultural, or economic niche. As it happens, we have some laws on the books that might help us achieve such a condition.[4]

REVOLUTION AND DEVOLUTION

Some might object that the Articles of Confederation were tried and failed. The question is, in what respect did they fail? Between 1783 and 1789, each state set up its own rules, often imposing tariffs or trade restrictions on neighboring states. The new Constitution, which went into effect in 1789, banned such trade policies. Otherwise, after Shay's Rebellion, the big question among some of the powdered wigs had been: *How would the colonies put down uprisings?* Unsurprisingly, Alexander Hamilton, that great lover of central authority, was among those most worried. Jefferson, on the other hand, saw the people's right to dissent as an important check on power:

> What country before ever existed a century and half without a rebellion? And what country can preserve its liberties if their rulers are not warned from time to time that their people preserve the spirit of resistance? Let them take arms.[5]

Hamilton won the debate. But Jefferson had been correct. And even though this volume is a call to nonviolent resistance, we know that, in some circumstances, we rabble have had to meet force with force.

But times change. We have to be careful to select just what kind of counterforce is appropriate. Maybe violent revolutions are unnecessary if we can find peaceful ways to engage in civil disobedience. Are there bottom-up ways to decentralize? We have the means at our disposal to fashion a robust system that allows for plenty of checks and escape hatches. Following the letter of the law, debates over the proper size and role of the federal government could be over. Each new jurisdiction would have to prove itself. Fifty experiments would allow us all to vote with our U-Hauls. Things could get even more interesting if we transitioned more federal or state powers to the counties.

A LESS PERFECT UNION

Such a system would be a step in creating a more antifragile condition. As urbanist Vince Graham put the matter,

> I am, at the Fed level, libertarian; at the state level, Republican; at the local level, Democrat; and at the family and friends level, a socialist. If that saying doesn't convince you of the fatuousness of left vs. right labels, nothing will.[6]

Nicolas Nassim Taleb poached the above quip for his book *Antifragile*. The idea is ideological experiments shouldn't result in system-wide catastrophes. Instead, we ought to "go local" with our pieties.

California's failures should remain with California. New York's with New York. Such a system would disabuse us of the urge to think of our political ideals as something to be forced down the throats of 350 million souls. California could spend lavishly on its failed policies, and Texans would no longer be forced to subsidize any of it.

Instead of a monstrous federal government imposing its capricious will, each jurisdiction would have to use what Dierdre McCloskey calls "sweet talk"[7] to persuade more folks into their dominion. This way, we could try out more experiments in living while insulating more people from the dangers of centralization.

Some of these jurisdictions might lean toward theocracy. Some might lean toward socialism. A few, perhaps, might be genuinely free. As long as each serves its members wisely, leaving a right of exit—so be it. Indeed, some of these experiments might include jurisdictions not affixed to a territory. The more systems there are, the more likely one can find something closer to the right fit.

Alas, too many incentives keep the current system in place. So it's time to break up. Decentralization is the light at the end of a very dark tunnel for America. Eventually, we may not have a choice but to dissolve the union—and at that stage, a breakup might be far uglier and more painful than one that is the product of rational agreement.

OPERATIONALIZING CONSENT

To repeat, the competitive dynamics of system diversity would become a great discovery process: a governance market. Imagine a kaleidoscopic array of possibilities for human betterment. At the very least, it would allow one to live according to her own principles within a general framework of rights and responsibilities enshrined in the common law. We could resolve our conflicts and solve our problems if we recognized the justice of a consent-based order.

Thomas Jefferson was a radical and still is by today's standards. But his radicalism was rooted in skepticism. Sadly, the world seems to have been enchanted by Alexander

Hamilton with his love of big banks, great powers, and Broadway shows—all of which have set our Republic on a path to ruin.

Instead of "systems thinking" and other technocratic fever dreams foisted on us by the proxies of the administrative state, we need stark, simple rules. We need less voice and more exit. Instead of activist judges, packed courts, and progressive policies, we need to let people try out all their goofiest ideas *at the most local level feasible.* Catholics call that subsidiarity. Political theorists call it federalism. Darwinians? Evolution through devolution.

There are a hundred ways to skin the decentralist cat.

The most familiar way is already written in the Constitution. We would need only a popular uprising to enforce it and live within its auspices.

The powers not delegated to the United States by the Constitution, nor prohibited by it to the states, are reserved to the states respectively, or to the people.[8]

That's the Tenth Amendment. It's been dead for more than a century. How might we resurrect it?

THE LIVING CONSTITUTION IS SUICIDE

An army of constitutional-law grads is waiting to tell us why the authorities may summarily ignore the plain text of these amendments, which are vital constraints on federal power. Otherwise, damn the General Welfare clause and similar loopholes, which the powerful use as bludgeons against the Bill of Rights.

For more than a century, so-called "living constitutionalists" have used their curious rationale to make up jurisprudence so that the powerful can do whatever they please. Though 90 percent of what the U.S. federal government does is unconstitutional under common-sense construals, plenty of well-paid silver-tongued lawyers say otherwise.

The professoriat is the worst.

Speaking of the devil, the execrable Woodrow Wilson once said of the Constitution:

> Society is a living organism and must obey the laws of life, not of mechanics; it must develop. All that progressives ask or desire is permission – in an era when "development," "evolution," is the scientific word – to interpret the Constitution according to the Darwinian principle; all they ask is recognition of the fact that a nation is a living thing and not a machine.[9]

Wilson is correct that society is no machine. While Mussolini might have been delighted at such claptrap, society is not an organism either. Society is an ecosystem. Like the Amazon rainforest or the Great Barrier Reef, society evolves.

But evolution happens by changes to combinations of DNA, even though the constituents of DNA are always the same, that is, some combination of adenine, guanine, cytosine, and thymine (AGCT). Evolution and emergence in the social realm are the products of simple rules, too. Social complexity depends on protocol simplicity. To be fair, Woodrow Wilson died before Watson and Crick discovered DNA. Yet it's clear the Technocrat-in-Chief wanted to direct society's development by replacing our constitutional DNA with Intelligent Design—all while appealing to Darwin.

By contrast, framer James Madison saw the Constitutional order as being built on a scaffolding of laws, with some being more fundamental than others. The most basic of these was a Constitution, which ought to be thought of as nigh-immutable. According to Madison, a Constitution "is established by the people and unalterable by the government, and the law [is] established by the government and alterable by the government." Such protocols would have to be simple, stable, and secure. Something as flimsy as fiat rule would become vulnerable.

As we suggested elsewhere: *Humans aren't smart enough.*

Wilson, like the progressives he fathered, was at odds with Madison. Like many Living Constitutionalists, far from viewing the Constitution as a relatively fixed set of protocols forged in the pragmatism of principle, Wilson saw the Constitution as an obstacle to his designs. Something so fixed could not be molded to his will. According to Wilson, Madison treated the Constitution as something mechanistic and inflexible. But Wilson could not simply discard it. So he would have to interpret it in a light different from that revealed in its plain text. In Wilson's view, such an interpretation would allow a nation to develop in a manner Darwin would have appreciated. Wilson was wrong.

While writing this chapter, I asked the artificial intelligence (AI) program ChatGPT to imagine a debate between Woodrow Wilson and James Madison, even though they were not contemporaries. Here is the result:

Woodrow Wilson: *The U.S. Constitution is a flawed document that has failed to keep pace with the changing* *needs of our society. It was written over 200 years ago, in a completely different time and place, and it no longer reflects the realities of the modern world. We need to move beyond the Constitution and create a new system of government that is more responsive to the needs of our people.*

James Madison: *The U.S. Constitution is a masterpiece of political thought that has stood the test of time. It was designed to protect the rights of the individual and limit the power of the government, and it has served us well for over two centuries. We should be careful not to throw out the Constitution simply because it is old. Instead, we should work to preserve its principles and adapt them to the challenges of the modern world.*

Woodrow Wilson: *The Constitution may have worked well in the past, but it is no longer fit for purpose. It is too rigid and inflexible, and it fails to provide the flexibility and adaptability that we need in a rapidly changing world. We need a new system of government that is more responsive to the needs of our people and more able to address the challenges of the twenty-first century.*

James Madison: *The Constitution may not be perfect, but it has proven to be a remarkably resilient document. It has survived wars, economic crises, and political upheaval, and it continues to provide a framework for our government and a safeguard for our rights. We should be careful not to abandon the Constitution simply because it is not perfect. Instead, we should work to preserve its core principles and adapt them to changing circumstances.*

Woodrow Wilson: *The Constitution may have served us well in the past, but it is no longer sufficient to*

*meet the challenges of the modern world. We need a new
system of government that is more responsive to the needs
of our people and more able to address the complex issues
that we face today. We cannot simply cling to the past
and hope that the Constitution will continue to work for
us. We must embrace change and move forward into the
future.*

James Madison: *The Constitution may not be
perfect, but it is still the best system of government that
we have. It provides a framework for ordered liberty and
protects the rights of the individual. We should be careful
not to throw out the Constitution simply because it is not
perfect. Instead, we should work to preserve its core
principles and adapt them to changing circumstances, so
that it continues to serve us well in the future.*

I was gobsmacked when I first read this result, not just
because the AI was impressive, despite some redundancy. It
seems sufficient to capture each figure's position.

THE OTHER SPECTRUM

In a similar spirit, let's imagine a spectrum x that goes *not* from
the progressive left to the conservative right but rather y that
goes from liberal to authoritarian. On such an axis, one can
plot the positions of relevant historical figures thus:

Spooner	Jefferson	Madison	Hamilton	Wilson	FDR
				∧	
LIBERAL				AUTHORITARIAN	

Ideally, it's time to move the slider in the direction of Lysander Spooner, which would probably be ideal. Jefferson or Madison would do, though. If you are wondering about Spooner, he was an abolitionist and legal theorist who worked in the nineteenth century. Like Jefferson, he was keenly interested in a doctrine of *consent*, writing,

"If any man's money can be taken by a so-called government, without his personal consent, all his other rights are taken with it; for with his money the government can, and will, hire soldiers to stand over him, compel him to submit to its arbitrary will, and kill him if he resists."

Spooner counts as more liberal than Jefferson, not merely because he openly deplored the institution of slavery. Spooner also thought that monopolies, particularly government monopolies, were only good for monopolists:

Universal experience attests that government establishments cannot keep pace with private enterprize [sic] in matters of business—(and the transmission of letters is a mere matter of business.) Private enterprise has always the most active physical powers, and the most ingenious mental ones. It is constantly increasing its speed, and simplifying and cheapening its operations. But government functionaries, secure in the enjoyment of warm nests, large salaries, official honors and power, and presidential smiles—all of which they are sure of so long as they are the partisans of the President—feel few quickening impulses to labor, and are altogether too independent and dignified personages to move at the speed that commercial interests require. They take office to enjoy its honors and emoluments, not to get their living by the sweat of their brows.[10]

Spooner despised government monopolies so much that he even tried to set up a competitor to the U.S. Postal Service (a monopoly of letter carriers). The government promptly shut the venture down. Later, Spooner got personal experience in the politicization of the Post Office, which used its monopoly powers to prevent abolitionist literature being sent to the South.

Happily, Spooner got to see the end of slavery. He did not, however, get to see the end of the federal government as a monopolist. While Spooner is correct that the State is generally torpid and corrupt in the execution of its duties, we must recognize how swift and strong central authorities can be when smiting down a competitor.

We are the competitors.

As we set about using entrepreneurial means to break up America's monopoly on governance, we must use all the tools the twenty-first century has to offer. And we must lock arms in solidarity. Or as Benjamin Franklin said as the Founders prepared to sign the Declaration, "We must all hang together, or, most assuredly, we shall all hang separately."

PART THREE
ACTIONS

11

THE REVOLUTIONARY TRIGGER

Justice is nothing other than the advantage of the stronger.
—Thrasymachus[1]

THE DECLARATION of Independence is a fading memory. Where once it was revered as the secular foundation of a people, it is now seen mainly as a curiosity that, at best, justifies an annual rite of fireworks and potato salad. For a few of us, though, the Declaration[2] remains a beacon. It flickers as a candle on a stormy night.

The most stirring passage urges us to claim our rights to "Life, Liberty, and the Pursuit of Happiness," but those rights seem sadly alienable today. Complementary passages remind us of what we must do in the face of tyranny. Yet, the tree of liberty[3] stands before us, molting and desiccated.

Legal scholar Randy Barnett argues Americans should treat

the Declaration as a charter document as weighty as the Constitution:

[T]he Declaration was considered to be a legal document by which the revolutionaries justified their actions and explained why they were not truly traitors. It represented, as it were, a literal indictment of the Crown and Parliament, in the very same way that criminals are now publicly indicted for their alleged crimes by grand juries representing "the People."[4]

The Executive has other ideas.

"If you wanted or if you think you need to have weapons to take on the government," said America's aged president, "you need F-15s and maybe some nuclear weapons."[5]

In some ways, President Biden was not wrong. He was just channeling Thrasymachus. But if Professor Barnett is right, we have a duty to confront a vital, but uncomfortable, question: at what point must Americans take it upon ourselves to revolt?

In other words: What is the revolutionary trigger?

PLAIN TEXT

Before howls of "Insurrectionist!" issue from ventriloquist dummies, I refer to a legal document that, at the very least, warrants seditious questions. Indeed, we're duty-bound to question authority, whether or not the Declaration is a proto-charter. Under such conditions, another American Revolution might seem paradoxical.

Revolution is in our DNA.

So let us explore the revolutionary code. I'll move through the relevant passages and discuss matters as I go.

That to secure these rights, Governments are instituted among Men, deriving their just powers from the consent of the governed[6]

The consent of the governed. Only those inculcated by state authorities' official civics books could argue that democratic voting is consent, much less that submission to power is consent.

In his book *When All Else Fails: The Ethics of Resistance to State Injustice,* philosopher Jason Brennan argues that there is no theory of state authority, nor special immunity, without gaping holes that must be filled with F-15s, nukes, and a supportive bandwagon of hooligans. He writes:

[If] governments do indeed have authority, it seems like there should be some morally relevant property or set of properties that explains why governments have authority. (...) If there is such a property, then it seems plausible that people should be able to identify it.[7]

Brennan adds that scholars have spent a lot of time and energy trying *unsuccessfully* to identify that property, and he comes with the receipts.

But what about voters? Brennan adds:

[W]e have good grounds to think that people would believe in government authority even if governments have no such authority. Empirical work generally finds we have a psychological bias to ascribe authority to others, even in cases where there clearly isn't any. Governments do everything in their power to reinforce that bias.[8]

Biases aren't mind-independent properties.

So, what sort of "property" is Brennan looking for? Most people aren't terribly attuned to such philosophical questions, so we imagine a concrete situation in which one is looking for a good doctor. In some limited sense, a physician is one who has skills and experience treating patients. Her skills and experience are bound up in her reputation for successfully treating people. If one is choosing a doctor, it doesn't take us to philosophical depths to imagine that skills and experience are properties relevant to making that choice.

But in cases where one does *not* choose some authority, we have to find some property that justifies the authority's exercise of power over the person in the absence of choice. And that property remains elusive. I suspect many, if not most people, just have an inborn submission instinct. Such an instinct might have helped human groups survive in the distant past. But one would have to show precisely how submission to some authority confers this type of benefit today.

Couple submission instincts with the fact that authorities feed us a steady diet of civic mythology around voting and elections. This creates a veneer of justification. Alas, voting is little more than a cheap Lotto ticket for partisans. That is— unless you happen to live in a swing state—the odds your vote will amount to anything are low. But even if you did vote in a swing state, voting is still not consent.

At best, voting expresses a preference. If your candidate loses, that's more obviously not consent. But even if your candidate wins, you are only expressing a preference about who shall have authority over you, which is blurred among the preferences of others. It is certainly not a decision about whether that authority ought to be empowered at all. Of course, if you do not vote at all, that's not consent, either. That you *could have* voted doesn't help matters. As legal theorist Lysander Spooner famously pointed out, if you found yourself conscripted into a war and given a gun, you might very well find yourself shooting at the enemy. Would your participation, then, demonstrate that you consent to be placed in this situation? Of course not.

Without consent, though, there are no just powers.

That whenever any Form of Government becomes destructive of these ends, it is the Right of the People to alter or to abolish it, and to institute new Government, laying its foundation on such principles and organizing its powers in such form, as to them shall seem most likely to effect their Safety and Happiness.[9]

In the absence of just powers, we should have the legal right to alter or abolish our government.

But our great and mighty government officials have other ideas.

One might argue that absent any formal consent mechanism our system allows representatives to alter (amend) the Constitution, which would *alter* the government at least. But such representation would be neither legitimate nor effective if one thinks of the Declaration as the law. My aim here is not to persuade you that we can oblige officials to view the Declaration as an enforceable legal document conferring certain rights. That would be dandy. Instead, it is to argue that the American experiment is failing and, though we got close, we need somehow to reboot.

We can no longer deny that our system of government has become *destructive* of those proverbial *ends*. So doesn't it need to be abolished? Maybe we have become accustomed to, inured to, this corrupted form. But Jefferson, et al., offer a cautionary note:

Prudence, indeed, will dictate that Governments long established should not be changed for light and transient causes; and accordingly all experience hath shewn, that mankind are more disposed to suffer, while evils are sufferable, than to right themselves by abolishing the forms to which they are accustomed.[10]

Acknowledging the dictates of prudence, I'm no more calling for the destruction of Chesterton's fence than I am fomenting Jacobin behavior. If there is any weight to the idea that our current assessment is a light or transient cause, I would ask how long a slave should be accustomed to the master's lash before he is justified in taking flight. If you don't like such extreme comparisons, how long must our list of grievances be? How long must we endure? As we'll see, the Founders offered an answer.

But first, is there any doubt that the Constitution has

become a dead letter? Our government officials are corrupt. States' rights are attenuated. And our federal system is a negative-sum game run by profiteers and sociopaths. So:

[W]hen a long train of abuses and usurpations, pursuing invariably the same Object evinces a design to reduce them under absolute Despotism, it is their right, it is their duty, to throw off such Government, and to provide new Guards for their future security.[11]

There you have it, in plain text.

One might argue that today's "long train of abuses and usurpations" doesn't hold up compared to the colonists' grievances. We will see. In the Afterword, I will list a series of grievances I think is no less justifiable than those enumerated by the early patriots. If even a only few of these rise to the level of abuse the colonists suffered under King George III, we must ask: What, if not any number of these, counts as a revolutionary trigger?

COURAGE AND NEW GUARDS

As the U.S. government continues its efforts to sinoform America, across the Pacific brave Chinese dissidents are showing the way despite terrible odds:

For Beijingers whose morning commute takes them under the Sitong overpass on the hectic north section of the city's Third Ring Road, October 13th, 2022, will live long in the memory. That was the day that plumes of smoke from a bridge fire drew their attention to two large crimson-daubed banners. One read: "Food, not nucleic acid tests. Freedom, not lockdown. Dignity, not lies. Reform, not Cultural Revolution. Votes, not leaders. Be citizens, not slaves."[12]

The ancients reminded us that courage is not the absence of fear. Aristotle said that fear fuels courage, or at least what impels us to act despite being afraid. As those Chinese dissidents challenged the Chinese Communist Party, we know they had to find courage, perhaps channeling desperation.

Thrasymachus's words still haunt us, though. The police powers of the United States government are mighty, too, so "justice" might amount to nothing more than the advantage of the stronger. Curiously, it didn't take "F-15s" or "nuclear weapons" for Pashtun cave dwellers to get the world's greatest fighting force out of Afghanistan. Whatever one thinks of the Taliban, I don't know many ordinary Americans with their courage.

Like many who admire the Declaration of Independence, I resist violence. After all, other human beings are sacred. I accept that they have a right to life, liberty, and the rest. But I also need my fellow human beings to reciprocate. If they do not, we have a problem. Therefore, like Buddhist warrior monks, we are not pacifists. If we must defend ourselves, we will. So we have to establish some clear threshold of mass self-defense—lines authorities cannot cross without repercussions.

When is it appropriate to counter abuses and usurpations with violence? Such is an important question, and I suspect answers will cross the domains of morality and strategy.

My hope is we need no violence at all.

By way of foreshadowing, in *The Decentralist*, I write:

We have to adopt that mien of silent, dogged resistance. Wherever possible, we have to drag our feet, refuse to comply, and make the costs of enforcement too high for authorities.

Next, we have to practice satyagraha. This Sanskrit word means roughly "truth force," and Mahatma Gandhi taught his followers to use satyagraha against the British Raj. The Freedom Riders and Civil Rights activists used similar tactics in the Jim Crow South. Satyagraha is thus a nonviolent means, even as it exerts enormous pressure against powerful hierarchies.

Today we have technological tools that Gandhi or MLK never had. So in practicing satyagraha, we must do so through the best available means....[13]

An army of software developers obsessed with self-government is sowing the seeds of change. They're designing ironclad institutions instead of declaring them by fiat and force. Many early experiments will fail. But some will succeed, and massive constituencies will form around those successes.

But until any revolutionary moment (or evolutionary process) arrives, we must figure out who our new Guards will be and what will keep them from turning into Gollums. In the meantime, we must write a new American story, all while we draw a line in the sand. That new story should include a shadow Constitution—one without all the loopholes that both progressives and populists have used to leave the current document in tatters. As Jefferson warned just six months before his death:

Under the power to regulate commerce, they assume indefinitely that also over agriculture and manufactures, and call it regulation to take the earnings of one of these branches of industry, and that too the most depressed, and put them into the pockets of the other, the most flourishing of all.[14]

He continues forthrightly, referring to the General Welfare clause as "sophistry" that opens the door to "whatsoever they shall think, or pretend will be for the general welfare."

The Living Constitution has been a sophist's playground.

As one who likes to keep his eyes on the horizon, I sometimes hesitate to look back. But posterity demands that we look to the past and the future. History has important lessons for us—including the rudiments of that distinctly American story. We must do everything we can to form a culture around that story, even as we rewrite it in the age of pixels. Otherwise, we will only be remembered as another fallen empire. Our cosmopolitan ideals will be lost. If we fail to pass the torch of *legitimacy in consent* to a new generation, our children and children's children will suffer under some yoke placed around their backs in the name of the general welfare. Indeed, maybe it's time a few of us came together to reimagine our great charter. Every great civilization needs its sacred texts. The Declaration of Independence remains such a text. It can fit nicely into a canon that includes an upgraded rulebook for the New Guards.

If you are awake and alert in this liminal age, you realize those New Guards might just be us.

12

ANYTHING THAT'S PEACEFUL

We can underthrow the state one contract at a time.
—Michael P. Gibson[1]

SEVEN YEARS before Karl Marx published *das Kapital*, a little-known Belgian liberal published an essay that might be the most important idea in political philosophy. Few know about Paul Emile De Puydt's panarchy, but more might want to learn about it. A challenge is embedded there, designed to prime your intuition pump. It goes like this:

What if you could live in your favorite system of government and keep your political opponents from obstructing your plans?

We can imagine this possibility, but with a twist.

In de Puydt's formulation, each community would open a membership office. A citizen would then be responsible for filling in a form and signing an agreement, as follows:

Question: What form of government would you desire?

Quite freely you would answer monarchy, or democracy, or any other.

Anyway, whatever your reply, your answer would be entered in a register arranged for this purpose; and once registered, unless you withdrew your declaration, observing due legal form and process, you would thereby become either a royal subject or citizen of the republic. Thereafter you would in no way be involved with anyone else's government. You would obey your own leaders, your own laws, and your own regulations. You would pay neither more nor less, but morally it would be a completely different situation.

Ultimately, everyone would live in his own individual political community, quite as if there were not another, nay, ten other, political communities nearby, each having its own contributors too.[2]

See the challenge?

You can live under any political system you like without leaving your driveway. The twist, though, is that you would join a civil association rather than a political party. Instead of crying your teardrop into the ocean and expecting the tide to turn (voting), you would dig a well with others in your community (membership). Instead of voting for a party, you would agree to live under a civil association's auspices for a subscription period. And if you didn't like the association, you would be free to leave after satisfying any conditions of the agreement.

In such a system, ideologues would have to eat their own dog food instead of serving it to you.

"It turns out there's only one thing that guarantees production of good laws," writes author Michael P. Gibson:

The people bound by the laws have to agree to be bound by them. Not hypothetically or tacitly, as in some imaginary will of the people or behind a veil of ignorance. Consent must be real, transparent, and continuous. A law can bind a single person only when and because that person consents to be bound by that law. All laws must be strictly opt in. Lawmakers could be saints, devils, or monkeys on typewriters—doesn't matter. The opt-out opt-in system lets only good laws survive. Bad laws are driven out of production.[3]

With an actual social contract, you can sign it or not. The only cost of this quantum leap forward is this: You cannot force anyone to join your association. That means you would have to tolerate the idea that many people will join other associations, just as, presumably, you tolerate the fact that people live in other countries.

People in different civil associations will have friction and disagreement. Happily, though, we have inherited the Common Law. Here's De Puydt again:

If a disagreement came about between subjects of different governments, or between one government and a subject of another, it would simply be a matter of observing the principles hitherto observed between neighboring peaceful States; and if a gap were found, it could be filled without difficulties by [appeal to] human rights and all other possible rights. Anything else would be the business of ordinary courts of justice.[4]

While we may agree that "human rights" is an ambiguous phrase, we interpret de Puydt as saying that innocent people should be protected from abuse or involuntary servitude. Without such assurances, few would be likely to join a given association.

More egalitarian-minded types will worry that all the rich people would flee their chosen association or form their own— leaving their association's less wealthy members to care for the poor. While some wealthy people engage in tax avoidance strategies, from offshore accounts to jurisdiction-hopping, most do not. Indeed, super wealthy people often engage in what evolutionary biologists call *costly signaling*, publicly visible sacrifices designed to attract mates or display status.

Though it's cheap to say so, some billionaires claim they want to be taxed more. Of course, it's not as if nothing can be done about it. People who say this are playing political games. They are always free to write a check to the U.S. Treasury at any time. They don't. (Call this revealed moral preference.) Billionaires such as George Soros, Tom Steyer, and Jeffrey Katzenberg are party loyalists. And if the voting patterns of the wealthy are any indication, plenty of rich people are probably willing to tolerate higher tax rates and are willing to pay for systems intended to help the poor. It would be a rather adolescent form of compassion if a rich person only wanted to pay higher taxes if others were similarly compelled.

Those who oppose compulsory wealth distribution think

delivering aid to the poor via bureaucratic authorities is ineffective and inhumane. So, even as some oppose government welfare, most want to relieve poverty through different means. Some efforts might start as local experiments but get replicated and scaled. Mutual aid recommends itself.

Our hypothesis is that governance pluralism, competition among civil associations, is far more likely to generate better governance and, therefore, better outcomes. As statesman Charles de Brouckère wrote of his contemporary's proposal:

---

de Puydt [has furnished] an outline of a system that would have the advantage of submitting the industry of security production, otherwise known as governments, to a competition as complete as that in which manufacturers of fabrics, for example, engage in a country under free trade, and achieves this without having recourse to revolutions, barricades, or even the smallest act of violence.[5]

The competitive dynamics of diverse systems would be a discovery process for better governance. At the very least, it would allow one to live according to her principles. Within a general framework of rights and responsibilities enshrined in the common law, something like de Puydt's panarchy is both possible and desirable.

THE CENTRALIST'S DILEMMA

Philosopher Robert Nozick warned of what he called "imperialistic utopians" who seek "the forcing of everyone into one pattern of community." Nozick, perhaps an inheritor of de

Puydt's challenge, sets out an argument for governance pluralism in his magisterial work, *Anarchy, State and Utopia.*[6]

So for imperialistic utopians, let's call them Centralists for short, the question becomes: How do you justify something as arbitrary as being born on this patch of soil or that to determine which set of rules you must comply with? For those committed to supreme, centralized authorities—there seem to be two possible paths:

> *x*: There is one single conception of the good that everyone in the world must embrace, no matter where in the world they live.
>
> *y*: Once one moves to another jurisdiction, he must live by its rules. As long as they are peaceful and have done no wrong, he is out of reach by the former jurisdiction.

I used to think most people would choose *y*. After all, if a system is attractive, people will want to join it. These days, however, I'm not so sure. Consider this passage from the World Economic Forum (WEF):

> The world must act jointly and swiftly to revamp all aspects of our societies and economies, from education to social contracts and working conditions. Every country, from the United States to China, must participate, and every industry, from oil and gas to tech, must be transformed. In short, we need a "Great Reset" of capitalism.[7]

These powerful aspirations are but the aspirations of the powerful.

Couched in language that seems innocuous at first, the watchwords of global corporatism are hiding in plain sight. For example, how does "the world" act to revamp anything? It doesn't. The powerful do. What is a "social contract"? It's certainly not something you sign. To the WEF, it's something you submit to. If every country "must participate," what are the consequences of defection? Countries don't act, either. People do. Such weasel words mask unholy intercourse between corporations and governments. We used to use the f-word to describe that offspring. As author Sheldon Richman reminds us, "fascism is socialism with a capitalist veneer."[8]

In short, where true liberalism separates corporations from the state, corporatism combines them. Public-private partnerships represent the unholy union of market power and political power. Fascism is the offspring.

ANYTHING PEACEFUL

Illiberal activists will use the human failings of the Founders to invalidate their ideals. Thomas Jefferson owned slaves and sired multiple children with at least one. He also died indebted, and these weren't his only sins. He failed to live up to his ideals. But liberalism's enemies don't care as much about the sins of the fathers as using tactics to discredit them. They want to distract us from the timeless urgency of liberal ideals.

As should be plain from its root, "liberal" indicates one who values freedom. Such is not the freedom to act with impunity, for example, to use Gyges's Ring to plunder a village. Instead, it is freedom limited only by the freedom of others. Edge cases can be tricky for courtrooms and classrooms alike, but the liberal ideal is to maximize freedom and minimize the coercion of humans by humans. My favorite formulation, short and sweet, comes from writer Leonard Read:

"Let anyone do anything he pleases, so long as it is peaceful."[9]

Of course, we must balance freedom against responsibility. But true liberals—call them original liberals—believe that human freedom should extend as far as possible, even if that means we must *choose* to adopt constraints or to make sacrifices for the community's good. Flanked as we are on either side by moralist progressives and conservatives, original liberalism makes room for different conceptions of the good. But this kind of toleration is asymmetrical. That is, both progressivism and conservatism are doctrines of moral *imposition*. For example:

Progressivism: The state must enforce *compassion* through compulsion and taxation.

Conservatism: The state must enforce *clean living* and *family values* through coercion.

Once one appreciates morality cannot be imposed, i.e., people must practice it, he or she will experience the gravity of liberalism as a fundamentally moral doctrine.

In focusing too much on political means, partisan progressives and conservatives alike tend to be half-arsed with respect to moral practice. So, *a pox on both*, I say. Now of course such a curse shouldn't imply there are no liberals who hold either strong progressive or conservative *personal values*. Those liberals exist. They're just rare. We should respect both their values and their rarity. We should also lock arms with those whose values don't require illiberal means. We need our contemporary liberalism to be ecumenical. To think otherwise would be to misunderstand liberal doctrine or to contribute to its demise.

There is a lot of room under the *anything-that's-peaceful* tent.

THE ONE TRUE WAY

As societies became more complex due to decentralized production and trade, intellectuals started to think that society would have to be ordered administratively. American elites looked to European intellectuals for alternatives to Anglo-American liberal democracy. Despite all the twentieth-century's horrors, many still do. The very idea of organic, locally-grown societies just seemed too chaotic. It's also more difficult to set yourself up as a technocrat in a consent-based order. Not only could an administrative class seek to justify central authority, but they could also clamber for positions at the top of any power pyramid.

A grand contest among different types of national hierarchies marked the twentieth century. Fascist brownshirts fought socialist redshirts in the streets even though these two ideologies were practically siblings. Throw in a few democides and a couple of World Wars: you have the makings of the world's bloodiest century. The World Wars even warped Americans' vaunted republic into a centralized Empire ringed by various forms of crony capitalism whose surpluses would grease the gears of the war machine. Post-war democracies like Britain became client states, as did fallen enemies.

Today, however, those pyramidal systems are showing their cracks. Yet the frenzy of functionaries to ascend to the highest echelons of power grows stronger. Each party doubles down on illiberal control measures that reflect their respective interests. The left has cast its lot with redistribution and identity politics, which includes moralistic crusades, crocodile tears, and shaming mobs. The right has become merely reactionary—a crude, contrarian populism pushed along by nationalism and nostalgia for a time that never was. Both teams love the state for its wealth transfers because they can use the gains granted to them to buy various constituency groups. Neither seems interested in confronting the fact that U.S. debt stands at record levels.

Because each team still fancies theirs is the One True Way, they leave little room for diverse perspectives, much less consideration of other ways society might be organized. Titanic warfare has become an ongoing spectacle that distracts the rest of us from the promise of humane cooperation in a pluralistic order. It's time for us to seize that promise before it is lost.

If you think I'm being hyperbolic, remember that America's favorite French vacationer, Alexis de Tocqueville, warned us about "supreme power" back in 1835:

After having thus successively taken each member of the community in its powerful grasp and fashioned him at will, the supreme power then extends its arm over the whole community. It covers the surface of society with a network of small complicated rules, minute and uniform, through which the most original minds and the most energetic characters cannot penetrate, to rise above the crowd. The will of man is not shattered, but softened, bent, and guided; men are seldom forced by it to act, but they are constantly restrained from acting. Such a power does not destroy, but it prevents existence; it does not tyrannize, but it compresses, enervates, extinguishes, and stupefies a people, till each nation is reduced to nothing better than a flock of timid and industrious animals, of which the government is the shepherd.[10]

Some folks are perfectly happy to be treated as timid and industrious animals. Too many try to pull the rope because the ghouls keep telling them that, through democracy, you are the ones pulling the strings.

Electoral politics is an absurd game-theoretical construction, which essentially reduces to, "Vote harder next time." Somehow, that never works out. Democracy is an illusion designed to shroud that great power pyramid, even as we're all being compelled to build it higher. If we are ever able to finish throwing off the chains of servitude, we will have to do better than what has become of the July 4th holiday. Perhaps, like the exodus from Pharoah, we should mimic the Jews and sit around the table to tell the story annually for a thousand years.

TRICKLE-DOWN IDEOLOGY

It used to be that humanity practiced trickle-down ideology. That is, some pointy head would set out a theory about how society ought to be organized. That theory would trickle down, like a combustible liquid, into the minds of those who would eventually become its evangelists. The evangelists would evangelize until the theory would trickle down to revolutionaries holding lit matches.

Fueled by ideological fervor, mass movements moved like wildfires. Successful revolutionary leaders would reward themselves with power. Some were more virtuous than others. Still, those in power set about to put into practice what had been theory, with massive stakes and enormous consequences. Whether in the Bolshevik Revolution as the culmination of Marx, the French Revolution as the culmination of Rousseau, or the American Revolution as the culmination of Locke, trickle-down ideology was the primary mechanism of social change.

Perfectionist theories animated imperfect people to replace imperfect social orders with other imperfect social orders. Some worked better than others for a time. As a fan of the American Revolution, this realization is something of a bitter pill. Not only is my preferred revolution coming apart after 250 years, but it's also not altogether clear that trickle-down ideology works anymore.

Still, a happy paradox lives in liberalism, especially in our upgraded version.

When you increase the number of systems people can opt into, à la de Puydt, you reduce the costs of switching between systems. Taking the simplest example, if we imagine that the fifty U.S. states were more like countries, almost entirely free of federal constraints. One would find a higher probability of discovering a system more closely resembling her ideal system. It would therefore be less costly to migrate than if she had to leave the country entirely.

Yet voting with your boat is not the only way to change systems. Today we live in an era of cloud governance. Distributed ledger technologies allow us to tokenize new systems, and these systems need not be associated with any territory or country. As such, we are seeing how innovation blurs the line between legal and computer code and how innovation can sever the connection between jurisdiction and territory.

Just think about how millions of people migrate daily between fiat currencies and bitcoin. The latter has no country, no central bank, and requires no trust in God or government.

Cryptocurrencies are just the beginning. In time, the cost to exit any given system will likely go down as more options become available to people and we normalize the idea of subscription governance, decoupled from territory. Over time, these switching costs are likely to stabilize, but currently, the cost of leaving any given national jurisdiction is high. Revolution, of course, is expensive. Tomorrow's revolutions, however, might just be a matter of "forking the code,"[11] which would be decidedly less bloody and less costly than 1776, 1789, 1861, or 1917.

IRISH DEMOCRACY AND SATYAGRAHA

When you go into the voting booth, you might as well be sending your prayers to Washington. But how many times do those prayers get answered? Even if your candidate gets elected, he doesn't give you the policies you want. Hardly anyone is happy with the sausage that comes out of our legislatures, and they'd be downright disgusted if they saw how it gets made. So why don't we just oblige everyone to make and eat their own sausage?

First things first. Political scientist James C. Scott reminds us that:

> More regimes have been brought, piecemeal, to their knees by what was once called "Irish democracy," the silent, dogged resistance, withdrawal, and truculence of millions of ordinary people, than by revolutionary vanguards or rioting mobs.[12]

So first, we have to adopt that mien of silent, dogged resistance. Then, where possible, we must drag our feet, refuse to comply, and make enforcement costs too high for authorities.

Next, we have to practice *satyagraha*. Again, this Sanskrit word means roughly "truth force," and Mahatma Gandhi taught his followers to use *satyagraha* against the British Raj. The Freedom Riders and Civil Rights activists used similar tactics in the Jim Crow South. *Satyagraha* is nonviolent means, even as it exerts enormous pressure against powerful hierarchies.

Today we have technologies Gandhi could never dream of. In practicing *satyagraha*, we can use the best available means. Such includes discovering new opportunities for exit. I'm not just talking about voting with your feet, though that can be a fruitful approach. I'm also talking about voting with your money, which includes *voting for new kinds of money*. I'm also talking about entering new systems—the net effect will be to create new markets in governance.

Polymath Balaji Srinivasan makes a stark assessment, which I have edited lightly for this format. He tweets:

It isn't a straightforward tech vs. media thing anymore. It's centralized tech-and-media vs. decentralized tech-and-media. Fiat vs. crypto. Centralist vs. Decentralist. Speech control vs. freedom of speech. Surveillance vs. encryption. And the establishment vs. global disruption.[13]

It's no wonder Red and Blue want you to pick a team. They would like you divided, conquered, and transfixed by the spectacle. The real showdown will be between those who want to be free and those who seek control.

One of the basic questions of "good" law is whether people follow it. The better the laws within a system, the more likely people will try to migrate to that system or follow that set of laws. In this sense, it doesn't matter what any theorist considers justice, much less "social justice." We are entering an era of radical social experiments carried out on smaller scales than the revolutionary experiments of past centuries. Thus, in the post-ideological age, systems of justice and law will compete. If your system cannot keep people from running for the exits, your theory will fail like a bad restaurant.

And that is as it should be.

13
SUBVERSIVE INNOVATION

In our actual world, what corresponds to the model of possible worlds is a wide and diverse range of communities which people can enter if they are admitted, leave if they wish to, shape according to their wishes; a society in which utopian experimentation can be tried, different styles of life can be lived, and alternative visions of the good can be individually or jointly pursued.

—Robert Nozick, *Anarchy, State and Utopia*[1]

MOST STUDENTS of political philosophy have had some contact with Robert Nozick's *Anarchy, State and Utopia* (ASU)—specifically Part II. And for good reasons. Part II is essential because it sets out devastating critiques of competing moral-political doctrines and awakens our deepest intuitions about the coercion required to make those doctrines a reality.

Nevertheless, Part III: A Framework for Utopia

(henceforth Framework), I believe, is Nozick's most important contribution. Framework is certainly under-appreciated compared to familiar thought experiments about people giving up money to watch Wilt Chamberlain play basketball. However, my objective in persuading readers of Part III's importance is not to rearrange the philosophical canon for students. Instead, my goal is strategic. Nozick's Framework recommends a mindset that can inspire more *subversive innovators.*

If you're not familiar with Nozick's work, don't worry. I'll summarize some key points. We can situate Nozick's ideas squarely within the Jeffersonian tradition that animates this work.

Nozick's Framework, properly applied, offers those who share his ideological priors a sketch of how to liberate more people from power and poverty. Such a project is more valuable than arguing endlessly about ideal justice, so as to realize ideal justice is practically impossible.

Debates about minarchism or anarchism can distract us from more salient questions about how we create more markets in governance, despite the imposed Westphalian order. I suggest we reshuffle Nozick's thesis to transform his theoretical Framework into a practical mindset. Finally, we can use Framework as a strategic lens for spawning subversive innovations that promise each of us a society that comes closest to our ideals.

MINARCHY VS. ANARCHY: THE DEBATE IS LARGELY A DISTRACTION

Before getting into a theoretical inquiry about minarchism or anarchism, permit me to offer a brief overview of Nozick's rationale in Part III. It goes something like this: To the extent that there is a justifiable state monopoly on violence (Nozick's minarchist version), the framework's job is to facilitate the free formation of new communities, which we'll follow Nozick in calling utopias. Finding (or founding) a utopia is a discovery process. So the framework's function is more or less to protect the rights of individuals exiting and entering new utopias. Competition for members among utopias accelerates the discovery process and means that the utopias must serve their members sustainably to survive.

We can get lost in a series of questions about such a framework's details, including whether or to what extent the framework needs to be a monopoly, a coalition, or a confederation, or whether it could run on a set of governance protocols that we might consider anarchist by degree. Such arguments—like the wider debate between minarchists and anarchists—I contend are highly speculative and largely a distraction.

Nozick built almost the entirety of ASU on post-hoc rationalization of the following statement: "Individuals have rights, and there are things no person or group may do to them (without violating their rights)." We can interpret this statement as aspirational and normative without detouring into metaethics debates. Beyond moral suasion, I doubt Nozick thinks of rights as somehow inhering in people like a protective forcefield. Certainly, he would acknowledge that— whether or not rights exist *objectively*—powerful people will continue to act in ways that bring offense to less powerful people, despite moral suasion. They do, and they will.

My argument here is not designed to settle debates among academics in Abstractionland, much less to go toe-to-toe with someone as formidable as Nozick on matters of moral theory. Instead, I assume that Nozick and I share similar values, whatever their metaphysical status. Indeed, as he opens ASU,

Nozick starts with the Kantian presumption about rights, which we can safely interpret as something like the "sacredness of persons." I share this value. I hope you do, too. But Nozick doesn't try to justify that presumption in ASU and uses Part II instead to prime readers' intuition pumps about situations in which other theorists throw rights out the window. I will do something similar, but perhaps more attenuated: seek solidarity with others who share Nozick's values. In other words, if you don't value human freedom or don't think of individuals as sacred, this article might not interest you.

Nozick constructs ASU in a manner that he believes will limn an *ideal institutional substrate* to protect sacred persons. I am doing the same, only acknowledging more explicitly that we (those of us who practice a sacred-persons doctrine) are operating in a world filled with those hostile to our values, including the values of autonomy, property rights, and—indeed—the liberal sacredness of persons.

So we are not attempting, as Nozick perhaps was, to persuade those who are hostile to our values to consider a different political philosophy, even a pluralistic one like that in ASU. Instead, we are presuming the value of human freedom and the sacredness of persons. We seek to instantiate those values in a hostile world by offering people choices. And we employ practical means—especially *entrepreneurial* means. Some of those means will involve traditional arguments about ideal justice but will also involve marketing—or what economic historian Dierdre McCloskey refers to as "sweet talk." Still, we know that most of these arguments smash into the sturdy barricades that protect real political authority and its supplicants.

Indeed, the main problem with academic arguments about minimal states or anarchies tend to operate as if completely abstracted away from a world filled with politicians, corporate cronies, cultural baggage, and traditions extending backwards in time. Theorists tend to think and write as if it were feasible to get everyone, everywhere, to sit down and read their three-part essays, then be transported to some magical realm where societies can be spawned on a vast, empty green. Alas, the world is a patchwork of predators and powers with claims on nearly every patch of soil.

By this point, I hope you can see why debates about minarchism and anarchism are mostly a distraction—unless, that is, one's strategic focus employs *means* that are ostensibly minarchist or anarchist. Governance institutions, including any given person's Utopia, exist in a world of Hobbesian states with rabid supporters who have authoritarian bees in their bonnets. Arguments about ideal justice resemble those debates about how many angels can fit on the head of the proverbial pin. Our ideals are our North Star but may never be our destination. In that sense, we must sit more squarely in the reality that arguments about ideal justice do little to create utopias, much less a framework for Utopia. Instead, we must turn to strategic means to move toward our ideals, which are niches or zones—*systems*—for sacred persons that must be created in a hostile fitness landscape crawling with predators and parasites.

A FRAMEWORK FOR UTOPIA-BUILDING: RESHUFFLING PART III'S THESIS

The basic idea of Nozick's Framework is that some people have utopian aspirations, but they have inadequate knowledge to realize their idea of Utopia in a complex world. The only way to discover any given Utopia is for people to try fashioning it and inviting others to join. According to Nozick, accomplishing this requires some general set of procedures—

institutions—that make governance pluralism possible at all. To reiterate, it looks like this:

- Some people want to live in their idea of Utopia, even though those selfsame people have inadequate knowledge to achieve that utopia.
- People should be permitted to attempt to build their best approximation of Utopia so long as such attempts do not injure others in their parallel (peaceful) attempts.
- Framework is a theoretical construct that can and should be turned into a set of political institutions with pluralistic utopia-building as its mission.

From this, one might imagine institutional or constitutional designers busily setting out to instantiate the Framework in a body of law.

At this point, Nozick must surely be aware of the problem we suggested above, namely that there are authoritarians among us. They eat at the same restaurants. They vote. And they hold forth on social media every day. Nozick calls them "imperialistic utopians" who seek "the forcing of everyone into one pattern of community."[2] These utopians have no time for pluralism.

Apart from a small minority who might read this, I'd speculate that once you factor out the politically apathetic, most people can be referred to as "imperialistic utopians," even in the United States, which the Founders built on the ideas of freedom and pluralism. The media landscape provides ample evidence, however anecdotal, for such speculations. At the very least, we know that powerful authorities are likely to attack any framework such as the one Nozick imagines. In the United States, the 9th and 10th Amendments are our closest purported legal means of guaranteeing some measure of pluralism. But political operatives and lawyers with notions about a "living Constitution" rendered these Amendments inert long ago.

So what is to be done?

That's not a terribly philosophical question. Indeed, it's just the sort of questions philosophers routinely avoid. Nevertheless, I have asked it and will try to answer it. I will do so by appealing to Nozick's genius while reorienting it to strategic ends.

- Nozick wants people to pursue building their idea of Utopia through a scaffolding hospitable to pluralism, even though most people hold views that militate against the ideas expressed in Framework.
- Instead, Framework can serve as a *strategic* construct—niche carving—through which dissidents can pursue various utopia-building projects, despite obstacles.
- People who share our values should vigorously pursue the construction of their best approximation of Utopia, so long as such attempts do not injure others in their parallel (peaceful) attempts and they are aware of the risks that authoritarian powers present.

No doubt Nozick was doing his job by offering a philosophical case—not just about the facts of pluralism but also about the need for a pluralism-enabling framework.

In reordering Nozick's premises into a strategic framework of niche creation I call *subversive innovation*, I look around at the authoritarian powers in our midst. Then, I seek out weak joints or legal gray areas to exploit, in which one might apply a liberatory strategy or recruit new constituencies through entrepreneurial means. Carving niches means experimenting with new governance systems, however modest, hoping that these systems prevail in competition. Such is the delicate dance of dissidence.

ASYMPTOTIC ANARCHY: INNOVATION AND ENTREPRENEURSHIP ARE SUBVERSIVE ACTS

Asymptotic anarchy is a process that, through innovation and experimentation, might move us closer to an ideal, even if we never fully realize it. In mathematics, an asymptote is a line that a curve approaches as it heads toward infinity. We might call that curve "degrees of frictionless freedom." Metaphorically, we can represent the movement toward anarchy as a similar function toward an ideal state: We might move ever closer but never get there. The ideal state would be one in which humanity has eliminated the initiation of violence by one person against another and reduced the costs—to near zero—for any given person to exit a governance system that isn't serving her. We refer to this ideal state as "anarchy" because it means no rulers. In this condition, one can join any existing community or association. In short, all governance under anarchy is rooted in "the consent of the governed." Of course, one might consent to another's rule in such a condition, but the consent provision and a right of exit are basic to our ideal.

Now let's turn to the idea of transaction costs. The main issue with Nozick's theoretical Framework is that it doesn't offer a full accounting of such costs, which, to be fair, is probably not really philosophy's job. So it's up to us to figure out how to apply a revised Framework in our current circumstances. For example, the dominance hierarchies that reign today, even in our vaunted democratic republics, not only come with incentives for self-preservation and expansion, they also almost always come with legions of supplicants who depend on their influence or largesse. Public-choice theorists explore the dynamics of political authority's interactions with special interests. Of all the subdisciplines of political science, public choice is perhaps the most realistic, as it assumes that even political leaders are motivated by incentives, just like anyone else. So whenever we are considering any political event, we can always expect such incentives to be in play, lingering in the background.

In light of these real-world dynamics, if we *move towards* some ideal, we won't do so simply by imagining the new Framework as the ideal, although that can be helpful in *knowing our why*. We must also apply the reshuffled Framework as a strategic focus on a continuous process of asymptotic anarchy carried out by dissident innovators and entrepreneurs with diverse conceptions of the good. In these different conceptions lie *customer value propositions* associated with an alternative system the entrepreneur proposes.

Notice the term customer. Despite connotations of bourgeois materialism, I submit that the Framework-as-strategy mindset prompts subversive innovators to think of people as customers rather than citizens. Why? A citizen operates in the magisterium of *must* (politics) rather than the magisterium of *ought,* which includes both morality and markets. So, *you ought to do x because x is the right thing* is a moral claim, or *you ought to try product y* is a marketing claim. Both appeal to one's ability to choose. In the magisterium of must, that is, *you must pay for z or else,* authorities simply compel you. Thus, the transition from a citizen-centric mindset to a customer-centric mindset lies in your willingness to, first, remain in the domain of *ought,* and then serve people better by offering them something better through marketing.

According to management consultant Matt Gilliland:

> When the perceived (risk/time-discounted) benefits of switching to an alternative (system) exceed the perceived benefits of the status quo (system)—factoring in the perceived switching costs—people will switch to the alternative.[3]

We can translate this heuristic into a series of steps:

1. Create overwhelming value in an alternative system.
2. Expose the diminishing benefits of the status quo.
3. Reduce switching costs.
4. Change people's perceptions of the alternative relative to the status quo.
5. Serve customers well and continuously improve.

Now, consider a few examples of the above, which can serve as object lessons:

- Uber persuades billions to use their platforms instead of the taxi cartel.
- Poor performance and bad policies send parents to myriad educational alternatives.
- Satoshi Nakamoto offers the bitcoin network as an alternative to the fiat monetary system.

- Legal innovators set up a special economic zone in Honduras (Prospera), which has some of the least restrictive institutions on earth.

This handful of examples demonstrates subversive innovation. Notice in each example that there is some elbow room in what constitutes a "system." While none is perfect, each system iterates in its efforts to practice steps 1 through 5 in terms of customer focus. Each effort carves out a niche that offers one the option to *exit* a legacy system (à la Albert Hirschman) and *enter* an alternative system. In today's hostile environment, it might be quite difficult to do wholesale institution-building from scratch. There will be no Constitutional moment. Instead, each effort might be narrower but slice into some aspect of a more comprehensive status-quo institution.

But note that system-switching from the magisterium of *must* (politically-contrived system) to that of *ought* (market-derived system) is different from going from one market-derived system to another, such as when abandoning MySpace for Facebook, or Google for Presearch. In the latter such cases, *ceteris paribus*, the more desirable system wins out as the absence of new customers destroys the less-valued system. By contrast, politically contrived tax-and-transfer systems have a competitive advantage in that they can use compulsion to trundle along, despite mass defections and relatively poor performance. And those dependent on the status quo will go to great lengths to protect their systems and to sow seeds of doubt about nascent competitors.

That is why subversive innovators must be prepared for counterstrategy by vested interests with seemingly endless resources.

Specifically, the vested interests will:

1. Find ways to bolster and defend the entrenched
   system
2. Sow uncertainty and doubt about your alternative
   system
3. Attempt to raise your switching costs through
   political favor-seeking
4. Change people's perceptions of the alternative
   relative to the status quo
5. Maintain perceptions instead of making system
   improvements

In response to such counterstrategies, subversive
innovators won't be able to rely on the coercive apparatus of
the tax-and-transfer state. But they can rely on a commitment
to telling the truth. So, suppose the subversive innovator finds
herself in narrative warfare with her enemies. In that case, the
value she creates for customers is a truth that will be difficult
(though not impossible) to overcome. The subversive
innovator will simply have to create more value, and customers
can shout it from the rooftops.

Uber and Bitcoin entered the market without asking for
permission. Because they did, consumers got a taste of their
services before establishment cronies could pay lawmakers or
agitate for regulators to shut them down. Indeed, because
customers were able to get a taste of the value before anti-
competitive efforts were fully underway, those customers
became a forceful constituency for protecting the newcomers'
venture.

Now the question becomes: Can new legal systems gain
new customers before predatory authorities frustrate their
plans?

14

FROM SHADOW CONSTITUTION TO NETWORK STATE

"Where is the plan you are following, the blueprint?"
"We will show you when the working day is over,"
they answer.

Work stops at sunset. Darkness falls over the
building site. The sky is filled with stars. "There is the
blueprint," they say.

—Italo Calvino, from *Invisible Cities*[1]

BALAJI SRINIVASAN HAS DISTINGUISHED himself as a neurodivergent fount. Ideas and analyses pour out of him, even on bad days. He regales interviewers momently with acronyms and anecdotes as if on a modafinil drip. One time he melted Tim Ferriss's face for four hours, which is that podcaster's entire workweek. More recently, Srinivasan did a seven-hour interview marathon with the sleepy Lex Fridman.

If you've never heard of Srinivasan, you're living in a bubble. Such is not to suggest Srinivasan is immune to criticism, nor that his staccato communication style couldn't, at times, use more finesse. It is instead to acknowledge his genius.

Srinivasan is the best of what formerly could be said about Silicon Valley. Creativity. Innovation. Entrepreneurship. His gifts as a founder/implementer might be less apparent to those who only know him from his tweets. Srinivasan has co-founded three startups that were later sold. He's done stints as chief technology officer of Coinbase and general partner at Andreessen-Horowitz. But since Silicon Valley went all decadence and social justice, let's just say Srinivasan now represents the antithesis of what author Michael Gibson refers to as the "paper belt."[2] That sorry corridor, stretching from Washington, D.C. to Boston, deals in "newspapers, ads, money, and diplomas—all paper, all fading in power."

Balaji Srinivasan stands over that part of the world with a lit match.

THE NETWORK UNITED STATES

To those who have been in the startup-societies space for decades, the dynamics of exit and voice[3] are nothing new. Bob Haywood, for example, has done more to make special jurisdictions a reality than any living person, having a hand in creating Shenzen, Dubai, and many more. But Haywood is quietly effective, so he may never get the Nobel Peace Prize he deserves.

Balaji Srinivasan has become startup societies' most outspoken champion, a rogue intellectual spreading the gospel of competitive governance. Srinivasan's main contribution to the space is his insistence that new jurisdictions should start by networking people in the Cloud around a moral mission (Satoshi smiles).

That brings us to *The Network State*.[4]

Regarding his bestselling ebook, Srinivasan says he's written a how-to guide, not a manifesto. I'd like to think this book would qualify as a complementary manifesto. Still, the moral and political case for consent-based societies can get lost in memes, culture-warring, and horse-race politics.

Pamphleteers like me have more to do.

By this point, I assume you're on board with the great liberatory project of the Declaration of Independence, as it contains that consent provision, which is the *key* to governance futurism. Maybe you also see that America's other secular scripture, the Constitution, is in tatters.

Forming a network state could be an important avenue to a cosmopolitan tent revival of true liberalism, though with significant upgrades. Because Srinivasan intends for *The Network State* to function more as a content-free guide for forming network states, even illiberal ones, let's set aside our moral-political priors for the moment.

To operationalize any Jeffersonian fire, we should consider starting a network state. Srinivasan lays out a seven-step program for doing just that.

1. *Found a Startup Society*: Form an online community around some set of moral commitments.
2. *Organize it into a Group Capable of Collective Action:* Coordinate members for mutual benefit, mutual aid, and mission focus.
3. *Build Trust Offline and a Crypto-Economy Online*: Meet in person but build an internal crypto economy.
4. *Crowdfund physical nodes*: Crowdfund physical assets—from tracts of land to towns—to form the

bases of a community's "archipelago" on *terra firma*.

5. *Digitally connect physical communities*: Connect members to the physical nodes in the archipelago through digital passports and mixed-reality technologies.

6. *Conduct an on-chain census*: Keep an ongoing count of member growth, income, and real estate, on-chain, through cryptographic means.

7. *Gain diplomatic recognition*: Negotiate diplomatic recognition from surrounding legacy states until you have a viable network state.

Because forming a network state means reconstituting a mutual-aid sector against all the headwinds, it won't be easy.

Critics have pointed out, justifiably, that this seven-step program means network states will still be nested in the jurisdictions of the powerful. Moreover, the world's peoples already have to pay for their predatory states, which leaves meager surpluses to fund developing new institutions or mutual-aid arrangements. Recall that the New Deal, WWII, and Great Society programs crowded out America's robust mutual-aid sector. Today, the warfare-welfare state means the richest nations on earth are dog-paddling in a sea of red ink. Authorities will soon have no choice but to inflate, default, or tax us more, leaving citizens with fewer resources.

But nothing worth doing is ever easy.

The financial ruin of the U.S. government and its people could help catalyze a renaissance. This time, we will have subversive innovators to help us unite in mutual benefit and mutual aid as we refocus our efforts on creating an order rooted in peace, prosperity, and pluralism.

THREE STEPS

As promised, I return to this manifesto business, which we can think of as a convenient source of *mission, morality,* and *meaning.*

The *mission* is to constitute a truly consent-based order in which individuals can choose their governance systems according to their conception of the good. *Morality* is how we justify a consent-based order. The essence of liberalism is to reduce mass compulsion. The array of communities and associations that flow from the governed's consent confer *meaning,* too. As people coalesce around shared values, common needs, and collective action, they will participate in a truly pluralistic society: what John Stuart Mill called "experiments in living." Many will fail. A few will succeed.

Now I want to focus on the first three steps in the program to create a network state:

1. *Found a startup society.*
2. *Organize it into a group capable of collective action.*
3. *Build trust offline and a crypto-economy online.*

There is so much to do in these first three. We oughtn't bite off more than we can chew. In what follows, I want to articulate a vision for what this particular startup society is and does.

THE SHADOW CONSTITUTION

Our first order of business is to bring the most formidable, talented, and *aligned* people together to fashion a shadow constitution. *Shadow* has connotations of an alternative cabinet in a parliamentary system, but it also evokes something more clandestine. This novel constitution should take the best from the one that Americans currently have but realize the promise of consent. The shadow constitution should also offer greater clarity and remove passages that have enabled the chicanery of a "living Constitution." These legal loopholes have opened the door to errant illiberalism and dubious interpretations that have rendered the most important protocols inert. For example, the General Welfare clause has been a monstrous loophole for the powerful, while Amendments 9 and 10—designed to empower the people—are as good as dead. I suspect our mission might be to eventually encode the shadow constitution so that members become customers who live by the auspices they have chosen.

Such is the essence of the "consent of the governed."

I imagine pulling together the most amazing people, from captains of industry to liberal philosophers, constitutional scholars to bright influencers, who would work in cross-functional teams to reimagine a constitutional order and its protocols. Over time, this group would coalesce around the shadow constitution, effectively ratifying it, as Founding Members.

THE SHADOW SOCIETY

As the shadow constitution is being finalized, a team of implementers will assemble a basic membership infrastructure in the Cloud. Initially, membership would offer a sense of solidarity and modest benefits. At launch, new members would sign on to the new constitution as a condition of membership. Otherwise, signatories pledge allegiance to this new governance substrate and its embedded values.

The Founding Members would then use their considerable influence to attract more members. New members would immediately see value for their dues and efficacy in association, all within a framework that facilitates community participation and personal growth. The Freemasons aren't a bad comparison. The key here, though, is efficacy. Can the organization get things done? Do the members feel their participation is valued? Collective action can be challenging, but technology can help.

TEMPLES AND TOKENS

Though he advises us to start in the Cloud, Srinivasan knows that in-person intimacy is irreplaceable. It's hard to imagine the Masons or the Oddfellows hunched over smartphones for very long. Community is possible online, but members must earn deep love and trust through personal interactions that bind them to each other, sacralizing them in their commitment to the mission. Thus, a series of centers, perhaps a franchise of "temples," could represent the first seeds of the archipelago. These might function as meeting places crowdfunded through dominant assurance contracts.[5]

But that's not all.

As a scion of Satoshi Nakamoto, Srinivasan emphasizes using cryptographic tools and tokens to represent the shadow society's internal value flows. Such is wise, because fiat currencies are being debased by and for legacy powers and, at the same time, retooled for central surveillance and control (see, for example, central bank digital currencies, or CBDCs). We can imagine utility tokens that can be used only among members. Members might opt for technology *not* built on a blockchain but still secure and decentralized, such as Holochain.[6]

ONE GIANT LEAP

Since about 2008, I have been cheerleading for the idea that we *ought to* build a consent-based social order. I knew it would involve technologies that lateralize power relationships, but the protocol designers would have to share certain commitments. With *The Network State,* Balaji Srinivasan has written a startup manual. Those two different-but-overlapping domains—*ought to* and *how to*—might seem confusing at first. But together, they're a one-two punch against legacy powers.

Just as the bitcoin whitepaper was the how-to manual for starting a decentralized peer-to-peer currency network, it carried significant moral-political assumptions. In sketching a network state around a fundamental commitment to the *consent of the governed,* Srinivasan's *how-to* assumes the *ought-to* for manifesto scribblers like me. Executing the first three steps of the shadow society would be one giant leap for the future of consent-based governance.

Of course, no one can do it alone.

15

ON FORMING THE JEFFERSON SOCIETY

To attack the citadels built up on all sides against the human race by superstitions, despotisms, and prejudices, the Force must have a brain and a law. Then its deeds of daring produce permanent results, and there is real progress.

—Albert Pike[1]

WHO ARE those men in strange adornments hanging out in lodges? Are they a cult? What is the compass? The All-Seeing Eye? Whatever the symbolism, the impact of Freemasonry on the American experiment, from revolution to Western expansion, cannot be understated. Masons embodied specific cultural values and institutions, which allowed them to till the soil over vast territories. Their human networks would allow for more formal institutions to take hold later—Republican institutions.

By the middle of the eighteenth century, American colonists

had begun to demand more representation. Later, when the American experiment proved the rabble could self-govern, Republicanism spread throughout the Western world. The overlap between the masonic spirit and the Republican worldview had been vital because it reinforced the idea that *culture and technology lie upstream from politics*. At a time before the Internet, television, and Morse code, lodge networks allowed people with Enlightenment values to spread out, move away from the seats of authority, and experiment with a polycentric organization. This network generated enough virtuous men to outnumber the bandits and politicians—at least for a time.

Freemasons and other fraternal societies provided a social safety net well before the government created a monopoly on welfare. And, ultimately, Freemasonry provided a socio-cultural "technology" that laid the groundwork for a more decentralized, political infrastructure—relatively speaking. In other words, to unify a diverse people, you needed a quasi-religious framework, a social technology, that both transcended religion and included it.

Yet the American Revolution helped to rend the ancient fraternity into two functionally distinct orders: Republican and Imperial. The Republican Freemasons essentially carried on the tradition of social organization built on culture and a constitution. The Imperial masons evolved to support the ambitions of the British Empire. In this way, America arguably became the quintessential form of Masonic governance—a decentralized upgrade from what we might call the London Fork. By way of anachronism, the break between the colonies and Great Britain saw two different versions of the masonic "code" evolve. In both cases, Freemasonry had been deployed in very similar ways, but in the service of markedly different aims: *centralization* and *decentralization*.

Admittedly, the story of American Empire is not so different from the British Imperial story, but there is precedent to be found in masonic doctrine. And Freemasons were integral to America's liberatory movements.

THE ANDERSON CONSTITUTION

In 1734, forty-two years before his complicity in high treason against the Crown, Benjamin Franklin republished the Reverend Dr. John Anderson's Freemasonry Constitution in Philadelphia. Some say this document, later muted by powerful authorities, helped plant the seeds of revolution in America and France. That is strange given the following passage, which, at first blush, seems unambiguous:

A mason is a peaceable subject to the Civil Powers, wherever he resides or works, and is never to be concerned in plots and conspiracies against the peace and welfare of the Nation.

One wonders, then, why so many famous Freemasons, from Simón Bolívar to Ben Franklin, turned out to be revolutionaries. Maybe it's because Anderson left them a loophole:

[I]f a Brother should be a Rebel against the State, he is not to be countenanc'd in his Rebellion, however he may be pitied as an unhappy man; and, if convicted of no other Crime, though the loyal Brotherhood must and ought to disown his Rebellion, and give no

> Umbrage or Ground of political Jealousy to the
> Government for the time being; they cannot expel him
> from the Lodge and his Relation to it remains
> indefeasible.[2]

If we squint a little, we can see two important aspects of these passages from Rev. Dr. Anderson.

First, revolutionaries rebel against the unjust authority, not the nation (where nation just means *a people born here*). From the rebel's perspective, rebellion serves the nation. To the extent that the powerful undermine peace and welfare through acts of tyranny, the rebel's job is to make a final stand against institutionalized injustice. Or that is the story they tell themselves.

Second, Anderson's rules require members to avoid complicity in revolutions on lodge time but maintain a fraternal relationship with the rebel if he's otherwise a good man. Reading between the lines, we can interpret this as a declaration of neutrality designed to preserve solidarity among brothers who might otherwise align themselves with different races, countries, or constituencies.

Between Anderson's original constitution and the American Revolution, the relevant parties would have had Locke's Second Treatise (1689) on their minds, too:

> As Usurpation is the exercise of Power, which another
> hath a Right to; so Tyranny is the exercise of Power
> beyond Right, which no Body can have a Right to.
> And this is making use of the Power any one has in his
> hands; not for the good of those, who are under it, but
> for his own private separate Advantage.[3]

For the Masons of the time, civil authorities were supposed to guarantee a reasonable expression of fundamental rights and freedoms, not personal gratification. Anderson's Masons would have been popping their heads up again rather meekly in the wake of the Glorious Revolution. Those roiling years exemplified the quarrels over religion and nation that most Masons hoped to avoid. But this history, along with the emerging philosophical Enlightenment, would have shaped the minds of most any Freemason that came after.

That is, until 1815.

In that fateful year, the Grand Lodge of England updated its constitution, removing any clause protecting rebels from expulsion. The question is: Why? In general, the constitution typically outlines the rights, responsibilities, and obligations of its members, as well as the rules and procedures for conducting Masonic activities. It is possible that the removal of the rebel clause may have been understood as necessary to ensure the stability and unity of the organization, particularly if there had been concerns about internal divisions.

It is also possible that the change was made to bring the Grand Lodge's constitution in line with the values of the time, which placed heavy emphasis on Britons' commitment to Queen and Country at a time of global expansion and efforts to "civilize" various peoples on multiple continents. After all, Freemasonry was a popular organization in many parts of the British Empire, including India, Africa, and the Caribbean. Such does suggest the fraternity's officials made a conscious decision to define the organization as an extension of the British Empire.[4] Perhaps the Freemasons' egalitarian brotherhood was a double-edged sword. As more elites and royals integrated into its corpus, imperial power co-opted the Masons to some degree (no pun intended).

DWINDLING LIGHT

Now, if you were to ask people on the street today, they'd have mixed ideas about the ancient fraternity. Some think the Freemasons provide infrastructure for a global conspiracy. Others think good people want moral teaching, community, and rituals without religion. Yet others believe the Freemasons possess secret knowledge, which they use to control various institutions worldwide. All such claims are correct in some measure, or at least they *were*.

When referring to Freemasonry at a time when the sun never set on the British empire, or America was exporting Republicanism, they would certainly be right. While countries such as France were caught between the Vatican forces of central authority and the Masonic influence of decentralized Republicanism, anglophone countries remained firmly in the latter camp. Even Britain straddled Empire and Republic with a constitutional monarchy balanced against parliament, retaining vestiges of the common law.

But somewhere along the way, the light began to dwindle on both sides of the Atlantic. That is, the Freemasons were no longer a force for either centralization or decentralization. Though they retained their ancient rites of personal and moral development, their influence faded.

In doing research for *Underthrow*, I interviewed Justin Arman, a 32nd-degree Scottish Rite Mason and member of Manly P. Hall Allied Masonic Degrees No. 373.[5] Arman is keen to revive the ancient order as a moral and cultural force. He worries the Freemasons have been reduced functionally to a social club with dwindling membership and influence. Arman hopes to change that. But first, it takes understanding masonic history, he says.

"We're taught that conquest is military victory," said Arman, "but deeper lessons of time reveal that mere military conquest eventually ends up in rebellions."

To maintain control, conquerors had to implement successful public-relations campaigns and cultural reprogramming.

"To prevent revolts," Arman avers, "the powerful had to *rule people's minds.*"

Arman thinks Freemasonry was not just a brotherhood for cultivating virtue and mutual aid. It was a near-perfect social technology for inculcating various peoples with Western values to prime them for British hegemony. Joining scholars of Freemasonry such as Jessica Harland-Jacobs, Arman thinks the order co-evolved with the British Empire. In other words, Freemasonry did for Britannia what the Vatican had done for Spanish colonialism.

"The relationship between Freemasonry's meta-religious structure and the empire provided a powerful, effective feedback loop for those with imperial ambitions," Arman adds.

That is, until the British Empire went broke and imploded.

THE INGREDIENTS

I asked Arman what the Freemasons did historically to empower their membership. By way of paraphrases, here are his replies. The Masons:

1. *Provided initiatic experiences* allowing men to see one another as brothers through a mythic bond transcending blood and race—creating preconditions for mutual aid;

2. *Created a supranational identity*, a kind of universal citizenship around the values of brotherly love, pluralism, and cosmopolitanism;
3. *Ritualized the liberal arts and sciences*, creating a methodological justification for patterns and models of Western modernity;
4. *Exported enlightenment values* and civility to tame wild lands and define masculinity according to Western norms;
5. *Taught equality before a higher power*, a meta-religious framework aligned with the Judeo-Christian conception of God—which, in turn, helped to engender values such as equality before the law, Natural Rights, and limited government.

That last point may seem odd or contradictory until you realize that most of the American Founders, despite their anti-authoritarian leanings, were still under the intellectual sway of Thomas Hobbes. Even though the Founders were not too keen to live under the Crown, they planted the seeds of another empire against the objections of Jefferson and the Antifederalists. Why? Because they imagined only a powerful, central authority could guarantee freedom.

HOBBES'S GHOST

Philosopher Thomas Hobbes thought that some powerful central authority had to be the primary source of peace and social cohesion. Under his rationale, an ultimate dominator should control outbreaks of violence in unchecked domination games. A Leviathan serves as protector, checking the ambitions of men who would otherwise engage in advantage-taking or, worse, perpetual warfare. Sadly, Leviathan states always outgrow their role as protectors. Invariably, they become instruments of domination run by sociopaths, ideologues, or sociopathic ideologues.

Lockean Republicanism only augmented the logic of Leviathan. It didn't replace it. The Hobbesian calculation is that each citizen gives up some of his or her absolute freedom to a sovereign authority in exchange for protection. This is referred to as a social contract. Under the Lockean construal, citizens might introduce checks and balances as an insurance policy against tyranny, but they still had to hope that the Leviathan would rule in their interests. Otherwise, good intentions would be the only difference between a benevolent sovereign and a mafia boss. The American Founders not only shared such views but produced the Declaration of Independence as a kind of legal writ detailing their grievances against the Crown's behaviors, which had been both violative and numerous.

But time passed. The Freemasons continued to evolve. And so did Leviathan.

It's no wonder that most British thought of their empire as a benevolent force for expanding liberalism and virtue. Many still do. And this had not been a mere paradox. The British Empire was, in many ways, a force for good. It helped to eliminate slavery over great swathes of the world—in some places for the first time. The British also established healthy institutions in places like Hong Kong and other prosperous zones within the Commonwealth. Stories of excesses and oppression, such as the British Raj in India, are familiar. Still, the logic of Leviathan no doubt helped to justify the imperial project, for good or ill. But now we see that imperial social technologies are prone to corruption, insolvency, and cycles of decline.

FROM WANT TO NEED

As the great welfare-warfare states ascended in the twentieth century, visions of a liberal, cosmopolitan world order started to evaporate. That is, until 1945 when the American hegemon rose in the detritus of the crumbled British Empire and two world wars. By this stage, the Freemasons had become "a *want* rather than a *need*," according to Arman. He would like to see his order reinvent itself as a *need* again.

But what need, specifically?

"Centralized institutions are failing," he replied. "The public no longer trusts them. Partisanship creates incommensurable epistemic and moral lenses. A quiet civil war is brewing. And a series of crises plague the people. Because our fundamental worldviews diverge, we can't agree on a common ethos."

"So what is to be done?" I asked.

"We have to rebuild the Temple," he replied.

The masonic revival, and the revival of all fraternities, will depend on whether they can establish the preconditions of a new, more highly decentralized order. That depends on people embracing certain kinds of social technologies. Freemasons are *very* good at developing, using, and *exporting* social technologies.

As regards decentralization, Arman is speaking my language. Indeed, he's speaking Jefferson's language. But internal reform will be challenging for the fraternity. The Freemasons include a general prohibition on discussing politics, which helps maintain unity among people of different political parties and walks of life. Arman's decentralization thesis might be confused as such.

I never asked Arman whether his views risk making him some sort of apostate.

COLONIZING MINDS

The time has come to attack what the old American mason Albert Pike referred to as "superstitions, despotisms, and prejudices." I'm not persuaded that today's Freemasons, heavy with history and gaudy with tradition, can be the sole vector of underthrow. While I am endlessly fascinated with the organization and its mysteries, I am left hoping that men like Justin Arman can help the ancient society to become relevant again. Otherwise, the world needs new experiments—even if those borrow from proven Masonic social technologies.

Therefore, it's not enough to write a book. If I mean the words I wrote on these pages, I have to commit to more. I must do more to help people of conscience become a countervailing force. One drop of water is a drop. A thousand drops of water is a shower. A billion drops of water is a deluge. I hope you agree. If you do, I invite you to join me. I can't do it alone. I realize this might seem a bit strange: like *breaking the fourth literary wall*. A call to action belongs in sales emails, not in books. But if we want to get anything done in these times, this is one of the rules we have to toss. Another will be for fraternal societies to tolerate revolutionaries again.

Ironically, there is little evidence[6] to suggest that Thomas Jefferson was ever a Freemason or that he was even an honorary brother. Yet Justin Arman argues the order fully embraces the Declaration's author as a "great ambassador of Masonic governance." If Jefferson could have lived to appreciate the extent to which the Freemasons provided humus soil for germinating fellow revolutionaries and enlightenment dandies, perhaps he wouldn't snort at the idea of a Jefferson Society with masonic features. After all, today's Masons view the Declaration of Independence as a masonic document, which just goes to show, again, that the Freemasons can adapt to human exigencies through time.

Hopefully, by now, you have read my case for embracing a network-state approach—the seeds for a New America in the Cloud, à la Balaji Srinivasan. After all, underthrow isn't just about washing old things away. It's about offering something new. And in this case, it also happens to be about offering something timeless.

Imagine a fraternal, sororal, or unisex society that:

1. Provides initiatic experiences
2. Creates a supranational identity
3. Ritualizes reason in the liberal arts and sciences
4. Exports (and imports) upgraded liberal morality, timeless values, and ancient wisdom
5. Teaches fundamental dignity and equality, with or without a higher power

In what follows, I will sketch out tentative protocols for the formation of a Jefferson Society. My hope is that I can inspire a small group of peaceful revolutionaries to join me, if only to commiserate as we watch an empire buckle under its own weight.

THE PROBLEMS

Together, we are confronted with a set of interconnected crises, which I have detailed throughout this book:

1. Expansion of authoritarian control
2. Partisan tribalism and civil conflict
3. An unhealthy focus on national sensationalism instead of local efforts

4. Crisis of community and civil society
5. Generalized disorientation and want of life meaning

Many of these problems arise from the realities of modern life, such as our busy work schedules, screen addictions, and diminished involvement in churches and civic groups.

But they are also the consequences of decisions made by others long ago that were imposed upon us. If you're dubious, just ask yourself: Why is it illegal for you to negotiate the price of a loan? Why must you use a certain scrip on a certain patch of soil? Why must you pay taxes to enrich corporations seeking monsters to destroy? And why are you being forced to bankroll those who would censor you?

Human systems protocols can work for good or ill. Our struggle as human beings is, and will always be, striking a balance between preserving traditions or good rules while changing those that have outlived their usefulness. Finding the sweet spot requires both deliberation and experimentation— preferably at the local level.

It's no accident that people have begun to focus so zealously on politics as the primary mechanism of institutional change. Such a focus inclines people to tribalize and fight over the spoils of central authority. The energy that could go into a thousand local efforts pours into national spectacles. We have a lot of opinions about such spectacles, but almost no control over them. And this is the way authorities want it. Indeed, as people have turned away from religious and civil associations, they have lost community in the process. Without community, we become more dependent on distant authorities and unaccountable corporations colluding to exploit us.

WE CAN CHANGE THAT. THE PROTOCOLS

Our organization must start as a minimum viable product (MVP), such that we demonstrate the profound human hunger for *mission, morality, mutualism,* and *meaning.* The elements of that MVP will be implemented as a discovery process where our founders will use what works and leave what doesn't work behind.

Consider some of those elements.

Mission To institutionalize the Consent of the Governed for the peoples of the world. Our mission to realize a global consent-based order reflects the unrealized wisdom of the American Founders as a universal code. The Jefferson Society helps people understand:

- Our current centralized, authoritarian order has created vice and debt, and its institutions are crumbling,
- We have a responsibility to establish the preconditions for a more stable, decentralized order for our progeny, and
- We shall create parallel, cosmopolitan institutions in which people can self-organize based on their shared conceptions of the good.

The Jefferson Society provides frameworks and preparations for constituting a consent-based order. Just as the Freemasons helped central authorities provide a moral-spiritual basis for their rule, e.g., with Britain's imperial governance, the Jefferson Society will provide the moral basis for a *decentralized,* self-sufficient order. That order will be based on consent, not colonialism or compulsion.

MORALITY

The society's founders seek to establish a moral order within a networked fraternity, built around six primary "moral spheres." The six moral spheres are *nonviolence, integrity, compassion, stewardship, pluralism,* and *rationality.* When it comes to the spheres, we are committed to active, continuous practice. Moral practice will improve our members and everyone whose lives they touch.

MUTUALISM

Our organization shall apply principles of mutual aid to assist members in ascending as individuals, providers, community members, and professionals. We will apply some social technologies developed by fraternal orders to strengthen our mutualism. And we will integrate new social technologies through iterative, distributed processes, aka trial and error.

MEANING

Human beings have been chasing the question of what it all means since our species was capable of pondering its own existence. We're still in pursuit of meaning, just as we're still in pursuit of happiness. While meaning is fundamentally subjective, The Jefferson Society will offer social technologies that provide latticeworks of meaning-making, especially intersubjective meaning, which is meaning people share.

If I thought I could simply hand down anything more in terms of protocol design, like Moses with his tablets, I would. But this effort requires humility and collaboration. I repeat a mantra present elsewhere in this volume:

We trust the institutions we build and use together.

THE PILOT

Elements of any Jefferson Society ought to include fun and fellowship. Most secret societies were birthed in pubs, after all. I see no reason why any pilot couldn't start with cigars, whiskey, and good conversation. For many, these simple vices symbolize coming together in conspiracy, but they also lubricate in-person interaction.

In some ways, we have used technology to reduce ourselves to atomized avatars. The Jefferson Society can be a way out of the emptiness and ephemera of online interaction. Those familiar with my work know I am sanguine about innovation. But innovation should facilitate deeply human interactions, too, especially the kind that makes one willing to offer another the shirt off his back.

Therefore, any fraternal or sororal society should:

- Build counter-institutions rooted in consent-based governance and mutual aid
- Adopt better systems for decentralized communications
- Redirect resources from wants to needs, that is, from pomp to preparedness
- Work towards empowering members to provide for and protect each other in the event of a breakdown in economic security or law and order
- Become centers of development and deep learning for members

Kindred souls will notice our society's current spiritual starvation but also sense an inner yearning to draw near to others again.

Still, we seek neither sycophants nor opportunists. We seek

sovereign individuals willing to gather in solidarity around *mission, morality, mutualism,* and *meaning*. From there, we will develop our own rituals, our own strategies, and our own legacy of service. For that is the closest we may get to immortality.

THE SECOND DECLARATION

When in the course of human events, it becomes necessary for us to dissolve the political bands that tether us to arbitrary power—and to assume among the powers of the earth the separate and equal station to which Universal Morality entitles us—posterity demands we enumerate the injustices and declare our resolve.

We still hold these truths to be self-evident:

That all men are created equal, that they are endowed by their Creator with certain unalienable Rights, that among these are Life, Liberty and the pursuit of Happiness.

We understand these timeless words to mean that no one is justified in subordinating another who has caused no injury and that neither majoritarian mobs nor deliberative bodies may deny us our life, liberty, or pursuit of happiness.

Therefore, in peaceful solidarity, we declare our independence—again.

CONSENT

To secure our rights, the People must institute new governance systems, deriving our just powers from the consent of the governed.

Whenever any Form of Government becomes destructive of our ends, it is:

"[T]he Right of the People to alter or to abolish it, and to institute new Government, laying its foundation on such principles and organizing its powers in such form, as to them shall seem most likely to effect their Safety and Happiness."

We do not take the implications lightly.

Still, when a "long train of abuses and usurpations" creates a condition of subjugation, it is our right and our duty, "to throw off such Government, and to provide new Guards for [our] future security."

We have waited long enough for elected officials to reform themselves and our system. We have seen too little progress. So the time has come for the People to alter our systems of government.

But we are under no illusions: powerful authorities do not care about lofty appeals. We can no more swarm them with muskets than ignore their power. We must instead launch a million experiments in liberation. The history of governments, after all, is a history of repeated injuries by authorities who oppress the people for the ends of power.

Enough is enough.

INJUSTICES

Our grievances pertain to actions of unchecked power. Such actions include:

1. Taking from us without our consent and preventing us from governing ourselves
2. Denying us guarantees in the Bill of Rights, especially Amendments I, II, IV, V, VI, VIII, IX, and X.[1]
3. Threatening, regulating, and oppressing us, too often without legislation or due process
4. Lying to us and keeping secrets from us, while evading accountability
5. Dividing and disenfranchising us through the spectacles of partisan polarization and national elections
6. Seeking to control us, that is, to engineer society as if it were a machine and we were its cogs
7. Forcing us to subsidize failed agencies, systems, and institutions
8. Granting favors or subsidies to reward the powerful at the expense of the poor.
9. Threatening, attacking, and imprisoning those who share the truth about them, criminalizing both demands for accountability and peaceful dissent
10. Trading on and profiting from inside knowledge of the very laws they make
11. Feeding our fears to grow the military-industrial complex out of all reasonable proportion
12. Threatening to confiscate our means of defending ourselves from criminals and tyrants
13. Taxing us without legitimacy through currency manipulation
14. Conscripting the media and social platforms into deception, spin-doctoring, and censorship on their behalf

15. Assaulting our shared moral principles, common law, and Constitution
16. Spying on the People and denying us our privacy
17. Auctioning power to corporate bidders and horse-trading with our property to expand their power
18. Mandating commercial relationships or associations we would never choose otherwise
19. Creating corrupt monopsonies of scientific research
20. Declaring "wars" on the People for "crimes" that have no victim
21. Invading countries that represent no credible threat to the People or our pursuit of happiness
22. Using unlimited debt to buy votes and expand their power—thus burdening our children and grandchildren
23. Threatening legal action, heaping charges on us, or seizing our property without due process
24. Inculcating our children with illiberal doctrines, identity politics, or bankrupt ideologies
25. Claiming expertise and decision-making rights on matters about which they have insufficient knowledge
26. Forcing us to use their debased monies and prevent us from using our own monetary networks
27. Creating perverse, unintended effects by meddling in complex systems they don't fully understand
28. Oppressing us repeatedly in the name of the common good
29. Putting the interests of elites over the needs of the People
30. Obstructing our pursuits and diminishing our happiness

The purposes for which the People's government was constituted have been usurped. So we must set about building society anew.

RESOLUTIONS

Therefore, we resolve to:

1. Work towards a society based on the *consent of the governed*
2. Embrace community self-determination and self-governance, starting with the revival and enforcement of Amendments IX and X of our lost Constitution
3. Challenge all unjustifiable claims to authority by one person over another
4. Found, find, or fund new jurisdictions—on land, sea, or in the Cloud—where we can live in peace
5. Practice nonviolence, integrity, compassion, toleration, stewardship, and rationality—where practice means direct reflection and action, *not* outdated politics
6. Protect open inquiry and free expression in both their spirit and letter
7. Judge others by the content of their character, never by irrelevant, arbitrary, or superficial characteristics
8. Respect one another's religions, traditions, and practices, so long as they are peaceful
9. Require full transparency from anyone who claims authority
10. Exit systems that violate our privacy, sovereignty, or right to peaceful association

11. Build systems that protect our privacy, sovereignty, and peaceful association
12. Construct communities that better reckon with the increased complexity of the modern world, balanced against the constraints of our human nature
13. Construct sovereign networks of property, communication, finance, and currency
14. Organize superior, anti-authoritarian systems of charity and mutual aid
15. Create the means to protect our pursuit of happiness and life meaning
16. Take it upon ourselves to protect and steward our natural resources
17. Condemn and avoid theft via the inflationary and redistributive policies of national central banks
18. Practice nonviolent resistance but defend ourselves vigorously against all violent actors
19. Revive federalism, devolving political power as locally as is feasible, always towards true self-government
20. Become resilient as individuals, families, and communities—empowering ourselves
21. Exploit the weak joints and leverage points of all unjust hierarchies
22. Exit any platform, system, or organization that has been compromised by unjust power
23. Defend ourselves and those we love with the fervor of hornets
24. Renounce allegiances to the major political parties and their national election spectacles
25. Oblige regional and local governments to override national authorities

26. Operate parallel legal systems centered on restitution instead of retribution
27. Radiate goodwill in the practice of community-building and peace
28. Solve social problems with our creativity, innovation, and social entrepreneurship
29. Practice morality in thought, word, and deed, while expecting the same from leaders
30. Replace our cowardice with courage, our doubt with confidence, and our hesitation with dedication

SIGNATORIES

This Declaration evokes the spirit of 1776, but each of the injustices and resolutions listed is cosmopolitan, designed to challenge unjust, unchecked political power wherever it is found. The peoples of the world must overcome the submission instincts that keep us in the grip of fear. If freedom is our children's birthright, let it never be said we were weak.

Our mission unites us in strength.

We are about to enter an era of upheaval that is unprecedented in our lifetimes. As we move forward together in the solidarity of Gandhi's *satyagraha* and Jefferson's self-evident truths, let these principles unleash new experiments in peace, freedom, and self-government. Though human events draw our attention to struggles among great powers, the greatest struggle of our time is the People against an Axis of Unjust Authority. We must not idle as the powerful encircle us with tentacles of control, even if they do so in the name of national security or the common good. After all, "The Thing itself is the Abuse!"[2]

Instead, we will vote with our money and our feet. We will

rise up as peaceful, digital insurgents, write tomorrow's rules, and become practitioners of underthrow. We can do so by building new societies in the detritus of power politics. We start by lending our voices to the universal principles set out in this document.

Once we make our declaration, we shall begin our struggle anew.

JOIN UNDERTHROW

ACKNOWLEDGMENTS

Tim Ferris once said you're the average of the five people you keep around you. I guess I'm lucky in this regard, because those five have contributed enormously to various aspects of my work, and to this book in particular.

Justin Arman is one of the most talented, insightful people I have ever known. I have benefitted enormously from our friendship and conversations. Justin enjoys a cameo appearance in Chapter Fifteen as an interviewee, which allowed me to treat readers to inside knowledge of Freemasonry.

Jenny Clary is *Underthrow*'s typesetter and also happens to be the mother of our daughter Pia. Jenny's support extends far beyond the textual presentation we experience. She has endured my working on three books now. Yes, three. How she puts up with me I cannot say.

Rich Dalton's meticulous read-throughs helped me make great improvements to the experience. Rich calls 'em as he sees 'em, which prompts me to reword, rework, and rewrite to the high standards of discerning readers like you.

Peri Worrell's eagle eye helped me launch this volume with few errors and inconsistencies. I can only admire her attention to detail and overall proofreading abilities.

James Harrigan is my editor at the American Institute for Economic Research (AIER) where I write a column. He encouraged me to assemble this book based on some of my scattered articles. Despite James's occasional misanthropy, I cherish our friendship.

Sid Borders is my talented son who, having become a young man, has begun to engage me on the ideas of my work, as I have begun to engage him on his. You might say this is one of the greatest gifts of being a dad.

I would like to extend thanks to Conrad Ziebland, whose photography I shamelessly stole for the cover. Appreciation also goes to Muwaffaq Safti for his interest and support on building a Shadow Constitution. Colin Pape's continued support and friendship keeps wind in my sails.

Kind words and appreciation also go to Carl Oberg, Michael Porcelli, Emily Tilford, Jim Babka, Chris Rufer, Ann Hord-Heatherley, Trish Hord-Heatherley, Jean Roberts, Michael Bell, Michael P. Gibson, and Brian Robertson.

NOTES

INTRODUCTION

1. Some of the founders had become concerned after Shay's Rebellion.
2. "The Library of Congress >Exhibitions>Thomas Jefferson>Thomas Jefferson to William Smith," accessed February 26, 2023. https://www.loc.gov/exhibits/jefferson/105.html.
3. Voltairine de Cleyre, *Anarchism and American Traditions* (Chicago, The International Anarchist Publishing Committee of America, 1932). Available at: https://theanarchistlibrary.org/library/voltairine-de-cleyre-anarchism-and-american-traditions. Accessed February 26, 2023.
4. "Extract from Thomas Jefferson to Pierre Samuel Du Pont de Nemours," The Jefferson Monticello>Jefferson Quotes & Family Letters. Accessed February 26, 2023. https://tjrs.monticello.org/letter/246.
5. "From Thomas Jefferson to James Madison, 30 January 1787," Founders Online. Accessed February 26, 2023. https://founders.archives.gov/documents/Jefferson/01-11-02-0095.
6. Founders Online, "Jefferson to Madison."
7. Founders Online, "Jefferson to Madison."
8. Michael Strong, "Radical Social Entrepreneurs: An Introduction to Strong's Law," Explorers Foundation website, Accessed March 15, 2023. https://www.explorersfoundation.org/archive/strong-michael-rse-law.pdf.
9. Vincent Ostrom, The Political Theory of a Compound Republic: Designing the American Experiment. (San Francisco: ICS Press).
10. Ostrom, Compound Republic.
11. De Cleyre, *Anarchism and American Traditions*.
12. De Cleyre, *Anarchism and American Traditions*.
13. Mark Moore, *Localism*. (Pea Ridge, AR: Ridge Enterprises, 2013).
14. Linda Raeder, *Freedom and Political Order: Traditional American Thought and Practice*. (Lanham, Lexington Books, 2018).
15. Jeffrey Tucker, "Where Does the Term 'Libertarian' Come from, Anyway?" Foundation for Economic Education. Published online September 15, 2016. Accessed February 26, 2023. https://fee.org/articles/where-does-the-term-libertarian-come-from-anyway/.

1. THE CHURCH OF STATE

1. Jeffrey Jones, "U.S. Church Membership Falls Below Majority for First Time," Gallup website. Published March 29, 2021. Accessed February 28, 2023. https://news.gallup.com/poll/341963/church-membership-falls-below-majority-first-time.aspx.

2. POLITICS IS THE PATHOLOGY

1. Edmund Burke, *A Vindication of Natural Society*, (Indianapolis: Liberty Fund, Inc., 1982), (originally published 1756). Accessed March 10, 2023. Available online at: https://oll.libertyfund.org/title/burke-a-vindication-of-natural-society.
2. Max Borders, *The Decentralist: Mission, Morality, and Meaning in the Age of Crypto*. Austin: Social Evolution, 2022.
3. Max Borders, "The Best Defense Against Violence," American Institute for Economic Research website. Published September 13, 2021. Accessed February 28, 2023. https://www.aier.org/article/the-best-defense-against-violence/.
4. Ken Klippenstein, Lee Fang, "Truth Cops: Leaked Documents Outline DHS's Plans to Police Disinformation," *The Intercept* website. Published October 31, 2022. Accessed February 28, 2023. https://theintercept.com/2022/10/31/social-media-disinformation-dhs/.
5. "Politics Makes Us Worse," Libertarianism.org, Published September 14, 2012. Accessed February 28, 2023. https://www.libertarianism.org/publications/essays/politics-makes-us-worse.
6. "Politics Makes Us Worse", Libertarianism.org

3. THE GREAT AUTHORITARIAN ARMS RACE

1. Saul Alinsky, Rules for Radicals, (New York: Random House, 1971).
2. "Remarks by President Biden on the Continued Battle for the Soul of the Nation," The White House website. Published September 1, 2022. Accessed February 28, 2023. https://www.whitehouse.gov/briefing-room/speeches-remarks/2022/09/01/remarks-by-president-bidenon-the-continued-battle-for-the-soul-of-the-nation/.
3. Leni Riefenstahl was a filmmaker and propagandist for the Nazis during the Third Reich.
4. "Summary of Terrorism Threat to the United States," Dept. of Homeland Security, National Terrorism Advisory System Bulletin. Published November 30, 2022. Expires May 24, 2023. Accessed February 28, 2023.

https://www.dhs.gov/ntas/advisory/national-terrorism-advisory-system-bulletin-november-10-2021.

5. "The Tree of Liberty (Quotation)," The Jefferson Monticello website. Accessed February 28, 2023. https://www.monticello.org/research-education/thomas-jefferson-encyclopedia/tree-liberty-quotation/.

6. "Summary of Threat," Dept. of Homeland Security.

7. Sheldon Richman, "Fascism," The Econ Library website. Accessed February 28, 2023. https://www.econlib.org/library/Enc/Fascism.html.

8. Stephanie Slade, "Both Left and Right Are Converging on Authoritarianism," Reason website (from the October 2022 issue). Accessed February 28, 2023. https://reason.com/2022/09/13/the-authoritarian-convergence.

4. LUXURY BELIEFS DEATH SPIRAL

1. Veblen, Thorstein, *Theory of the Leisure Class*. (N.p.: Outlook Verlag, 2022), 112.

2. Rob Henderson, "Thorstein Veblen's Theory of the Leisure Class—A Status Update," published November 16, 2019, accessed March 1, 2023. https://quillette.com/2019/11/16/thorstein-veblens-theory-of-the-leisure-class-a-status-update/.

3. "Average public school teacher salary." USA Facts website, accessed March 1, 2023. https://usafacts.org/data/topics/people-society/education/k-12-education/public-school-teacher-salary-average/.

4. Dick Startz, "Do teachers work long hours?" Brookings Institution website, published June 12, 2019, accessed March 1, 2023. https://www.brookings.edu/blog/brown-center-chalkboard/2019/06/12/do-teachers-work-long-hours/.

5. Steve Albini (@electricalWSOP), Twitter post, published August 24, 2022, accessed March 1, 2023. https://twitter.com/electrical-WSOP/status/1562555768250937344.

6. John Halpin, "Americans Want the Federal Government To Help People in Need," Center for American Progress website, published March 10, 2021, accessed March 1, 2023. https://www.americanprogress.org/article/americans-want-federal-government-help-people-need/.

5. THE DEEP STATE IS BREAKING DOWN

1. "You can't handle the truth! (Jack Nicholson)," mavromedia Youtube channel. Published online June 25, 2011. Accessed March 2, 2023. https://youtu.be/MMzd40i8TfA.

2. Nicholas Schou, "How the CIA Hoodwinked Hollywood," The Atlantic website. Published July 14, 2016. Accessed March 2, 2023.

https://www.theatlantic.com/entertainment/archive/2016/07/operation-tinseltown-how-the-cia-manipulates-hollywood/491138/.

3. Nathan Maxwell, "FBI Targets Outspoken Parents, School Boards Silence Them," Institute for Free Speech website. Published June 9, 2022. Accessed March 2, 2023. https://www.ifs.org/blog/fbi-targets-outspoken-parents-school-boards-silence-them/

4. "You Can Read All the 'Twitter Files' Right Here," The Western Journal website. Published December 9, 2022. Accessed March 2, 2023. https://www.westernjournal.com/can-read-twitter-files-right/.

5. "You Can Read All the 'Twitter Files' Right Here," The Western Journal website. Published December 9, 2022. Accessed March 2, 2023. https://www.westernjournal.com/can-read-twitter-files-right/.

6. Joseph A Wulfsohn, "Jim Baker, ousted Twitter lawyer and ex-FBI official involved in Russiagate, was a CNN analyst in between jobs," Fox News website. Published December 8, 2022. Accessed March 2, 2023. https://www.foxnews.com/media/jim-baker-ousted-twitter-lawyer-ex-fbi-official-involved-russiagate-cnn-analyst-between-jobs.

7. Victor Nava, "Elon Musk fires Twitter lawyer James Baker over 'suppression' of documents on Hunter Biden story, New York Post website. Published December 6, 2022. Accessed March 2, 2023. https://nypost.com/2022/12/06/elon-musk-fires-twitter-lawyer-james-baker-over-hunter-biden/.

8. Melissa Koenig, "Controversial FBI agent Elvis Chan DENIES claim he warned Twitter security chief about Hunter Biden leak - as investigation reveals extent of FBI's tentacles in Silicon Valley," Dailymail.com website. Published December 21, 2022. Accessed March 2, 2023. https://www.dailymail.co.uk/news/article-11559535/FBI-agent-Elvis-Chan-DENIES-warned-Twitter-security-chief-Hunter-Biden-leak-operation.html.

9. Vivek Ramaswamy, Jed Rubenfeld, "Twitter Becomes a Tool of Government Censorship," Wall Street Journal website. Published August 17, 2022. Accessed March 2, 2023. https://www.wsj.com/articles/twitter-becomes-a-tool-of-government-censors-alex-berenson-twitter-facebook-ban-covid-misinformation-first-amendment-psaki-murthy-section-230-antitrust-11660732095.

10. Justin Hart, "The Twitter Blacklisting of Jay Bhattacharya," Wall Street Journal website. Published December 9, 2022. Accessed March 2, 2023. https://www.wsj.com/articles/the-twitter-blacklisting-of-jay-bhattacharya-medical-expert-covid-lockdown-stanford-doctor-shadow-banned-censorship-11670621083.

11. Phillip W Magness, James R Harrigan, "Fauci, Emails, and Some Alleged Science," American Institute for Economic Research website. Published December 19, 2021. Accessed March 2, 2023. https://www.aier.org/article/fauci-emails-and-some-alleged-science/.

12. "Elizabeth Warren asks Amazon to 'stop peddling misinformation about Covid vaccines and treatments'," New York Times website. Published September 8, 2021. Updated September 24, 2021. Accessed March 2,

2023.   https://www.nytimes.com/2021/09/08/world/elizabeth-warren-amazon-covid-misinformation.html.

13. U.S. Department of Justice, Office of the Inspector General, *Report of Investigation: Recovery of Text Message from Certain FBI Mobile Devices Redacted for Public Release*, 8. (Washington, D.C., OIG website, 2018). Accessed March 2, 2023. https://oig.justice.gov/reports/2018/i-2018-003523.pdf.

14. Republican Staff, *FBI WHISTLEBLOWERS: WHAT THEIR DISCLOSURES INDICATE ABOUT THE POLITICIZATION OF THE FBI AND JUSTICE DEPARTMENT*, 2. (Washington, D.C., U.S. House of Representatives Judiciary Committee, 2022). https://judiciary.-house.gov/sites/evo-subsites/republicans-judiciary.house.gov/files/lega-cy_files/wp-content/uploads/2022/11/HJC_STAFF_FBI_REPORT.pdf.

15. Elizabeth Elkind, "REVEALED: FBI warned Twitter about a 'hack-and-leak' operation targeting Hunter Biden in weekly 2020 meetings before the laptop story was censored," The Daily Mail website. Published December 5, 2022. Updated December 5, 2022. Accessed March 4, 2023. https://www.dailymail.co.uk/news/article-11503613/FBI-   warned-Twitter-hack-leak-operation-target-Hunter-Biden-2020-meetings.html.

16. Jim Clapper, et al., "Public statement on the Hunter Biden Emails," Politico website. Published October 19, 2020. Accessed March 4, 2023. https://www.politico.com/f/?id=00000175-4393-d7aa-af77-579f9b330000.

17. Ciaramella CJ, "It's (Almost) Always the Feds: How the FBI Fabricates Schemes to Entrap Would-Be Radicals," Reason website. Published September 9, 2022. Accessed March 4, 2023. https://reason.-com/2022/09/04/its-almost-always-the-feds/.

18. KanekoaTheGreat, "Elon Musk slams CISA censorship network as 'propaganda platform'," Kanekoa News website. Published December 28, 2022. Accessed March 4, 2023. https://kanekoa.substack.com/p/elon-musk-slams-cisa-censorship-network

19. Miranda Devine. "Ex-CIA Chief spills on how he got spies to write false Hunter Biden laptop letter to 'help Biden.'" *New York Post*, April 20, 2023.

20. Klippenstein, "Truth Cops."

21. Mike Benz, "Biden's National Science Foundation Has Pumped Nearly $40 Million Into Social Media Censorship Grants and Contracts," Foundation for Freedom Online website. Published November 22, 2022. Accessed March 4, 2023. https://foundationforfreedomonline.com/11-22-22.html.

22. Ryan Grimm, "LEE HARVEY OSWALD, THE CIA, AND LSD: NEW CLUES IN NEWLY DECLASSIFIED DOCUMENTS," The Intercept website. Published December 19, 2022. Accessed March 4, 2023. https://theintercept.com/2022/12/19/lee-harvey-oswald-cia-lsd-jfk/.

23. Whitney Webb, *One Nation Under Blackmail, Vol. 1* (2022, Walterville, Oregon, Trine Day).

24. Jordan Hall, "Understanding the Blue Church," Deep Code website. Published March 30, 2017. Accessed March 4, 2023. https://medium.com/deep-code/understanding-the-blue-church-e4781b2bd9b5.
25. Hall, "Blue Church."
26. Marti Gurri, "The Fifth Wave: Is the Medium Really the Message?" Discourse Magazine website. Published August 22, 2022. Accessed March 4, 2023. https://www.discoursemagazine.com/uncategorized/2022/08/22/the-fifth-wave-is-the-medium-really-the-message/.
27. Joe Lancaster, "A New FBI Building Would Cost Billions. Do We Even Need One?," Reason website. Published December 20. 2022. Accessed March 4, 2023. https://reason.com/2022/12/20/a-new-fbi-building-would-cost-billions-do-we-even-need-one/.

6. DON'T MESS WITH OUR ROOTS

1. Michael Strong, "Academia: the World's Leading Social Problem," James G Martin Center for Academic Renewal website. Published August 26, 2012. Accessed March 4, 2023. https://www.jamesgmartin.center/2012/08/academia-the-worlds-leading-social-problem/.
2. "Topics: Critical Race Theory," libertarianism.org website. Published December 9, 2021. Accessed March 4, 2023. https://www.libertarianism.org/topics/critical-race-theory.
3. "Politics Makes Us Worse," libertarianism.org website. Published September 14, 2021. Accessed March 4, 2023. https://www.libertarianism.org/publications/essays/politics-makes-us-worse.
4. Paul Kingsnorth, "The Abolition of Man (and Woman): Gender, Sex, and the Machine," The Abbey of Misrule website. Published July 14, 2022. Accessed March 4, 2023.
5. Lily Sánchez, "Why We Should Abolish the Family," Current Affairs website. Published September 5, 2022. Accessed March 4, 2023. https://www.currentaffairs.org/2022/09/why-we-should-abolish-the-family.
6. Alex Perez, "Spiral Dynamics: 8 Levels of Human Value Systems, by Clare W. Graves," About Happy Life website. Published October 12, 2020. Accessed March 4, 2023. https://abouthappylife.com/spiral-dynamics/.
7. Brooklyn Reece, "It's Time to Stop Saying 'Sir' and 'Ma'am'," An Injustice! website. Published August 14, 2020. Accessed March 4, 2023. https://aninjusticemag.com/its-time-to-stop-saying-sir-and-ma-am-868b049116cb.
8. Paul Kingsnorth, "The liberal order is already dead: Chaos will reign even if Putin retreats," Unherd website. Published February 17, 2022. Accessed March 4, 2023. https://unherd.com/2022/02/the-liberal-order-is-already-dead/.
9. Kingsnorth, "Liberal Order Already Dead."

10. Alexis de Tocqueville, *Democracy in America,* (1997, Virginia, American Studies Programs at the University of Virginia). Accessed March 4, 2023. https://xroads.virginia.edu/~Hyper/DETOC/ch2_05.htm.
11. Daniel B Kein, Dominic Pino, "Edmund Burke's Classical Liberalism," National Review website. Published July 28, 2022. Accessed March 4, 2023. https://www.nationalreview.com/magazine/2022/08/15/edmund-burkes-conservative-liberalism/.

7. TOO COMPLEX FOR MISSION CONTROL

1. Paul Krugman, "The Power of Biobabble," Slate website. Published October 24, 1997. Accessed March 5, 2023. https://slate.com/business/1997/10/the-power-of-biobabble.html.
2. F. A. Hayek, "The Use of Knowledge in Society" American Economic Review, XXXV, no. 4 (September 1945):519–30.
3. Evan Thomas, "Attack from the Left: Paul Krugman's Poison Pen," Newsweek website. Published March 27, 2009. Accessed March 5, 2023. https://www.newsweek.com/attack-left-paul-krugmans-poison-pen-76063
4. Stephanie Kelton, Rohan Grey, "How Do We Fix the Economy? Modern Monetary Theory, Explained," The Problem With John Stewart Youtube channel. Published February 24, 2022. Accessed March 5, 2023. https://www.youtube.com/watch?v=0G6obeUKWmw.
5. File Unemployment, "5 Ways to Build a Strong Economy," fileunemployment.org website. Updated February 10, 2021. Accessed March 5, 2023. https://fileunemployment.org/training-education/5-ways-to-build-a-strong-economy
6. Alexander Tziamalis, Amr Algarhi, "Labour are much better at running the economy than voters think – new research," The Conversation website. Published June 8, 2021. Accessed March 5, 2023. https://theconversation.com/labour-are-much-better-at-running-the-economy-than-voters-think-new-research-162368.
7. Larry Elliot, "The computer model that once explained the British economy," The Guardian website. Published May 8, 2008. Accessed March 5, 2023. https://www.theguardian.com/business/2008/may/08/bankofengland-governor.economics
8. George Selgin, William D Lastrapes, Lawrence H White, "Has the Fed been a failure?" *Journal of Macroeconomics* 34, no. 3 (September 2012):569-596 https://www.sciencedirect.com/science/article/abs/pii/S0164070412000304.

8. A LITTLE REBELLION NOW AND THEN
IS A GOOD THING

1. John Perry Barlow, "A Declaration of the Independence of Cyberspace," Electronic Frontier Foundation website. Published February 8, 1996. Accessed March 5, 2023. https://www.eff.org/cyberspace-independence.
2. Adam Thierer, "Exit, Voice, and Loyalty at 50: How a Classic Book Continues to Inspire," Cato Unbound website. Published August 10, 2020. Accessed March 5, 2023. https://www.cato-unbound.org/2020/08/10/adam-thierer/voice-exit-innovation/.
3. Yaneer Bar-Yam, "Teams: A Manifesto," Medium website. Published July 31, 2016. Accessed March 5, 2023. https://medium.com/complex-systems-channel/teams-a-manifesto-7490eab144fa.
4. Yaneer Bar-Yam, "Complexity rising: From human beings to human civilization, a complexity profile," in *Encyclopedia of Life Support Systems (EOLSS)* (Oxford, UK: EOLSS Publishers, 2002). Available online at:https://necsi.edu/complexity-rising-from-human-beings-to-human-civilization-a-complexity-profile.
5. Adam Thierer, *Permissionless Innovation and Public Policy: A 10-Point Blueprint* (Arlington, Virginia, Mercatus Center, 2016): Available at: https://permissionlessinnovation.org/wp-content/uploads/2016/04/PI_Blueprint_040716_final.pdf
6. Max Borders. *The Social Singularity* (Austin, Texas: Social Evolution, 2018).
7. If it wasn't clear, I refer to the U.S. Constitution
8. Jamie Bartlett, "Return of the city-state," Aeon website. Published September 5, 2017. Accessed March 5, 2023. https://aeon.co/essays/the-end-of-a-world-of-nation-states-may-be-upon-us.

9. CAN WE HAVE WELFARE WITHOUT
THE THREAT OF VIOLENCE?

1. Pyotr Kropotkin, *Mutual Aid: A Factor of Evolution* (1902): Chapter 2. Published online June 20, 2020. Accessed March 6, 2023. https://en.wikisource.org/wiki/Mutual_Aid:_A_Factor_of_Evolution/Chapter_II.
2. *Don Boudreaux, "The Hockey Stick of Human Prosperity," Marginal Revolution University, Everyday Economics course, video. Accessed March 6, 2023.* https://mru.org/courses/everyday-economics/trade-growth-hockey-stick-human-prosperity.
3. Deirdre McCloskey, "The Great Enrichment Was Built on Ideas, Not Capital," Foundation for Economic Education website. Published November 22, 2017. Accessed March 6, 2023. https://fee.org/articles/the-great-enrichment-was-built-on-ideas-not-capital/.

4. "Tanomoshiko," Wikipedia entry. Edited January 21, 2023 Accessed March 6, 2023. https://en.wikipedia.org/wiki/Tanomoshiko.

5. "List of regions by past GDP (PPP) per capita," Wikipedia entry. Edited on March 2, 2023. Accessed March 6, 2023. https://en.wikipedia.org/wiki/List_of_regions_by_past_GDP_(PPP)_per_capita.

6. Ihle Z Mtshali, Everything You Ever Wanted to Know About Those Sou-Sou Savings Clubs African and Caribbean Women Love, Essence website. Published December 6, 2020. https://www.essence.com/news/money-career/what-is-a-sou-sou-savings-club-facts/.

7. Alexis de Tocqueville, *Democracy in America, volume 2* (London: Longman, Green, Longman, and Roberts, 1835):128-9.

8. Robert Moffit and Peter Sperry, "From Mutual Aid to Welfare State: How Fraternal Societies Fought Poverty and Taught Character," Heritage Foundation website. Published July 27, 2000.

9. Chara Ranasinghe, "Global debt is fast approaching record $300 trillion–IIF," Reuters website. Published September 14, 2021. Accessed March 6, 2023. https://www.reuters.com/business/global-debt-is-fast-approaching-record-300-trillion-iif-2021-09-14/.

10. TRUST IS BUSTED. BUST THE TRUST

1. Woody Harrelson, "I'm an American tired of American lies," The Guardian website. Published October 17, 2002. Accessed March 6, 2023. https://www.theguardian.com/film/2002/oct/17/theatre.artsfeatures.

2. Michael Huemer, "The Problem of Authority," Cato Unbound website. Published March 4, 2013. Accessed March 6, 2023. https://www.cato-unbound.org/2013/03/04/michael-huemer/problem-authority/.

3. Aila Slisco, "Kathy Griffin Blasted for Saying to Vote Republican if You Want a Civil War," Newsweek website. Published September 6, 2022. Accessed March 6, 2023. https://www.newsweek.com/kathy-griffin-blasted-saying-vote-republican-if-you-want-civil-war-1740434.

4. Roger Pilon, "The Forgotten Ninth and Tenth Amendments," *Cato Policy Report*, Vol XIII, No. 5, September/October, 1991. Available online at: https://www.cato.org/sites/cato.org/files/serials/files/policy-report/1991/9/theforgottenninthandtenthamendments.pdf.

5. Library of Congress, "Thomas Jefferson to William Smith," Nov 13, 1787. https://www.loc.gov/exhibits/jefferson/105.html.

6. Nassim Taleb, *Skin in the Game* (Random House, 2018).

7. Deirdre N McCloskey, "Language and Interest in the Economy: A White Paper on 'Humanomics'" (2010). American Economic Association, Ten Years and Beyond: Economists Answer NSF's Call for Long-Term Research Agendas, Published August 12, 2011. Accessed March 6, 2023. https://ssrn.com/abstract=1889320.

8. "Rights Reserved to States or People," U.S. Constitution Center website. https://constitutioncenter.org/the-constitution/amend-

ments/amendment-x.

9. Woodrow Wilson, *The New Freedom* (New York: Doubleday, Page and Company, 1913). Available online at: https://www.gutenberg.org/files/14811/14811-h/14811-h.htm.

10. Lysander Spooner, "The Unconstitutionality of the Laws of Congress, prohibiting Private Mails" (1844). https://oll.libertyfund.org/title/spooner-the-unconstitutionality-of-the-laws-of-congress-prohibiting-private-mails-1844.

11. THE REVOLUTIONARY TRIGGER

1. "Callicles and Thrasymachus," Stanford Encyclopedia of Philosophy. Published Aug 11, 2004. Edited August 31, 2017. Accessed March 7, 2023. https://plato.stanford.edu/entries/callicles-thrasymachus/.

2. "Declaration of Independence: a transcription," The National Archives website. Accessed March 7, 2023. https://www.archives.gov/founding-docs/declaration-transcript.

3. "Tree of liberty (quotation)," The Jefferson Monticello website. Accessed March 7, 2023. https://www.monticello.org/research-education/thomas-jefferson-encyclopedia/tree-liberty-quotation/.

4. Randy Barnett, "What the Declaration of Independence Really Claimed," Washington Post website. Published July 4, 2015. Accessed March 7, 2023. https://www.washingtonpost.com/news/volokh-conspiracy/wp/2015/07/04/what-the-declaration-of-independence-really-claimed/.

5. "Biden: To Take On Government 'You Need F-15's And Maybe Some Nuclear Weapons'," Newsweek YouTube channel. Published June 24, 2021. Accessed March 7, 2023. https://www.youtube.com/watch?v=SHLHkmWoYDU.

6. "Declaration," National Archives.

7. Jason Brennan, *When All Else Fails: The Ethics of Resistance to State Injustice*, 206–38. (Princeton University Press, 2019).

8. Brennan, *When All Else Fails*.

9. "Declaration," National Archives.

10. "Declaration," National Archives.

11. "Declaration," National Archives.

12. Aaron Sarin, "A Single Spark," Quillette website. Published October 22, 2022. Accessed March 7, 2023. https://quillette.com/2022/10/26/a-single-spark/.

13. Aaron Sarin, "A Single Spark," Quillette website. Published October 22, 2022. Accessed March 7, 2023. https://quillette.com/2022/10/26/a-single-spark/.

14. "Jefferson on how Congress misuses the inter-state commerce and general welfare clauses to promote the centralization of power (1825)," Online Liberty Library website. Accessed March 7, 2023. https://oll.liberty-

fund.org/quote/jefferson-on-how-congress-misuses-the-inter-state-commerce-and-general-welfare-clauses-to-promote-the-centralization-of-power-1825.

12. ANYTHING THAT'S PEACEFUL

1. Michael P Gibson, "The Nakamoto Consensus—How We End Bad Governance," blog post. Published April 3, 2015. Accessed March 8, 2023. https://medium.com/@William_Blake/the-nakamoto-consensus-how-we-end-bad-governance-2d75b2fa1f65.
2. Paul-Emile de Puydt, *Panarchy* (1860), trans. John Zube, (NSW, Australia: Panarchy in our Time: 1998). Published online 2004. Accessed March 8, 2023. https://www.panarchy.org/depuydt/1860.eng.html.
3. Gibson, "Nakamoto Consensus."
4. DePuydt, *Panarchy*.
5. C.D.B., "Review of Panarchy by Paul-Émile de Puydt (1860)," Molinari Institute website. Accessed March 8, 2023. https://praxeology.net/CDB-PEDP-P.htm.
6. Robert Nozick, *Anarchy, State and Utopia* (Oxford: Blackwell Publishers, 1974), 319–320. https://archive.org/details/0001AnarchyStateAndUtopia/page/n1/mode/2up.
7. Klaus Schwab, "Now is the time for a 'great reset'," World Economic Forum website. Published June 3, 2020. Accessed March 8, 2023. https://www.weforum.org/agenda/2020/06/now-is-the-time-for-a-great-reset/.
8. Sheldon Richman, "Fascism," The Library of Economics and Liberty website. Accessed March 8, 2023. https://www.econlib.org/library/Enc/Fascism.html.
9. Leonard Read, "Anything That's Peaceful." Available online at https://www.amazon.com/Anything-Thats-Peaceful-Case-Market/dp/1452854165.
10. "Tocqueville on the form of despotism the government would assume in democratic America (1840)," Online Library of Liberty website. Accessed March 8, 2023. https://oll.libertyfund.org/quote/tocqueville-on-the-form-of-despotism-the-government-would-assume-in-democratic-america-1840.
11. "Justin Goro-The Great Hard Fork An Unraveling of State Legitimacy," Isuu website. Accessed March 8, 2023. https://issuu.com/jahari-belcher/docs/blockchain_hard_fork.
12. James C Scott. Two Cheers for Anarchism (Princeton: Princeton University Press, 2012).
13. Balaji Srinivasan (@balajis), "It isn't a straightforward tech vs. media thing anymore," Tweet, August 13, 2021. https://twitter.com/balajis/status/1426358902275203072

13. SUBVERSIVE INNOVATION

1. Nozick, *Anarchy, State and Utopia.*
2. Nozick, *Anarchy, State and Utopia, 319–320.*
3. Matt Gilliland, private communication, used by permission.

14. FROM SHADOW CONSTITUTION TO NETWORK STATE

1. Italo Calvino, *Invisible Cities,* trans. William Weaver (Orlando: Harcourt, 1974).
2. Michael Gibson, *Paper Belt on Fire: How Renegade Investors Sparked a Revolt Against the University* (New York: Encounter Books, 2022).
3. Wikipedia entry, "Exit, Voice, and Loyalty," Published May 11, 2005. Last edited February 16, 2023. Accessed March 10, 2023. https://en.wikipedia.org/wiki/Exit,_Voice,_and_Loyalty.
4. 1729, "The Network State in One Thousand Words," The Network State website. Accessed March 10, 2023. https://thenetworkstate.com/the-network-state-in-one-thousand-words.
5. Alex Tabarrok, "Dominant Assurance Contracts," Foresight Institute website. Published May 16, 2021. Accessed March 10, 2023. https://foresight.org/summary/dominant-assurance-contracts-alex-tabarrok-george-mason-university/.
6. "Why Holochain?" Holochain website. Accessed March 10, 2023. https://www.holochain.org/.

15. ON FORMING THE JEFFERSON SOCIETY

1. Albert Pike. Morals and Dogma of the Ancient and Accepted Scottish Rite of Freemasonry (1871). Accessed March 10, 2023. https://www.academia.edu/2622262/The_Constitutions_of_the_Free_Masons_1734_An_Online_Electronic_Edition.
2. John Locke, *The Second Treatise of Government* (London: A Millar and Associates, 1690). Published online April 22, 2003. Updated December 25, 2021. Accessed March 10, 2023. https://www.gutenberg.org/files/7370/7370-h/7370-h.htm.
3. Jessica Harland Jacobs. Builders of Empire: Freemasons and British Imperialism, 1717-1927 (Chapel Hill. University of North Carolina Press), 99.
4. Jessica Harland Jacobs. *Builders of Empire: Freemasons and British Imperialism, 1717-1927* (Chapel Hill: University of North Carolina Press,

2013), 99.
5. Disclosure: Justin Arman and I are close friends. I could not have written this chapter without his insights.
6. The Jefferson, "Fraternal Organizations." Accessed March 10, 2023. https://www.monticello.org/research-education/thomas-jefferson-encyclopedia/fraternal-organizations/.

THE SECOND DECLARATION

1. The U.S. Bill of Rights. Bill of Rights Institute website. Accessed March 11, 2023. https://www.billofrightsinstitute.org/primary-sources/bill-of-rights.
2. Edmund Burke, *A Vindication of Natural Society*, (Indianapolis: Liberty Fund, Inc., 1982), (originally published 1756). Accessed March 10, 2023. Available online at: https://oll.libertyfund.org/title/burke-a-vindication-of-natural-society.

www.ingramcontent.com/pod-product-compliance
Lightning Source LLC
Chambersburg PA
CBHW060449280326
41933CB00014B/2710